BLOOD AND
DNA EVIDENCE

For Terry, one of the "1817 Oak Street Boys,"
my kindred spirit . . . of Chevy engines, ducks, and more bubbly!

Acknowledgments

This book would not have become a reality without the loving support of my wife, Joan. In addition, she cheerfully supported the staging of many of the simulated blood spatter results in her kitchen! Thanks to Joe Elliot and Mathew Bacon of School Specialty, Inc., for their support. Special thanks to Ken Rando for helping with the electrons. Thank you to George J. Schiro, MS, DNA Technical Leader, Acadiana Criminalistics Laboratory, for his careful reading of the manuscript and many helpful comments and suggestions.

Library of Congress Cataloging-in-Publication Data

Rainis, Kenneth G.
    Blood & DNA evidence : crime-solving science experiments / Kenneth G. Rainis.
        p. cm. — (Forensic science experiments)
    Includes bibliographical references and index.
    ISBN-10: 0-7660-1958-6 (hardcover)
    ISBN-10: 0-7660-3171-3 (paperback)
        1. Bloodstains—Juvenile literature. 2. Forensic hematology—
Experiments—Juvenile literature. 3. DNA fingerprinting—Juvenile literature.
4. Forensic genetics—Experiments—Juvenile literature. I. Title.
    HV8077.5.B56R35 2006
    363.25'62–dc22   2005029214

ISBN-13: 978-0-7660-1958-4 (hardcover)
ISBN-13: 978-0-7660-3171-5 (paperback)

Printed in the United States of America

10 9 8 7 6 5 4 3

To Our Readers: We have done our best to make sure all Internet Addresses in this book were active and appropriate when we went to press. However, the author and the publisher have no control over and assume no liability for the material available on those Internet sites or on other Web sites they may link to. Any comments or suggestions can be sent by e-mail to comments@enslow.com or to the address on the back cover.

Every effort has been made to locate all copyright holders of material used in this book. If any errors or omissions have occurred, corrections will be made in future editions of this book.

Illustration Credits: All illustrations by Kenneth G. Rainis, except as follows: AP Wide World Photos, pp. 9, 20, 54, 74; The Biology Project, University of Arizona, p. 70; © 2006 Jupiterimages Corporation, p. 47; Private Collection, p. 7; © 2006 by Stephen Rountree (www.rountreegraphics.com), pp. 3, 15, 23, 36a, 42, 52.

Background Illustration Credits: Shutterstock.com (blood drops); Life Art image copyright 1998 Lippincott Williams & Wilkins. All rights reserved (DNA).

Cover Photo: © 2006 Jupiterimages Corporation (foreground); Shutterstock.com (background).

BLOOD AND DNA EVIDENCE

Crime-Solving Science Experiments

Kenneth G. Rainis

Science Consultant:

Brian Gestring, M.S.
Director of Forensic Science Program
Pace University
New York, New York

CONTENTS

CHAPTER 1

● ●

The Case of the Blood-Soaked Cloth

In 1994, Charlotte Stewart, a retired nurse, was found murdered in her Bronx apartment. The motive appeared to be robbery. Her wallet and checkbook were missing. There were no signs of forced entry. A bloody two-foot statue found at the scene was identified as the murder weapon. Nearby was a blood-soaked cloth. The police had few other leads, and Charlotte Stewart's case soon turned cold.

In 1989, Virginia and Florida started routinely collecting DNA from convicted criminals. (DNA is the genetic material inside the cells of organisms. You will learn more about it in Chapter 2.) More states followed throughout the years. This collected DNA is sent to labs to obtain DNA profiles. A DNA profile is a sort of identification code of who you are. Your DNA profile will be different from your friend's DNA profile because you each have different DNA in your cells.

The DNA profiles are stored electronically in a computer database. A database is a collection of information that is organized for a computer search. Computers compare an unknown DNA profile, such as one found at a crime scene, to known DNA profiles from individuals in the database. They look for a match.

In 1992, the Federal Bureau of Investigation (FBI) created CODIS—Combined DNA Index System. This system links all local and state DNA databases to FBI computers in Clarksburg, West Virginia.

Charlotte Stewart's death might have never been solved except that her murderer committed other crimes. As a convicted felon, his DNA profile had been entered into CODIS.

In Charlotte Stewart's case, the police had a bloody cloth from the murder scene to test. Police already knew, from other forensic test results, that the blood on

Law enforcement personnel have access to CODIS, a computer database that contains DNA records of many individuals.

the cloth did not come from the victim. Whose blood was it? In 2004, a DNA profile was developed from the collected blood. When authorities entered the profile into CODIS, they found a DNA profile match: forty-one-year-old Richard Jackson, Charlotte Stewart's nephew. Jackson had a criminal record of seven arrests. He had just been released from prison in April 2004, after serving nine years for a 1993 stabbing. Because he was a convicted felon, his DNA profile had been entered into CODIS.

Forensic DNA analysts carefully reviewed the computer match data. They confirmed the DNA profile match results. The fact that there were no signs of forced entry also agreed with the fact that Jackson was a relative. Apparently, burglary had ended in murder. Police arrested Jackson—ten years after Charlotte Stewart's death. They charged him with murder, and he received a life sentence without parole.

Blood and DNA Analysis

Forensic science is scientific information that is used during an investigation of a legal issue. The examination of blood and bloodstains provides the forensic scientist with useful information about a case. If stains are discovered at a crime scene, analysis can tell if these stains are blood, and if they are human. Bloodstain patterns are also studied. They can often reveal more

Forensic science is *scientific information* **that is used during an** *investigation* **of a legal issue.**

Scientists at the FBI DNA laboratory in Quantico, Virginia, follow careful methods to assure quality test results.

facts about what happened at a crime scene. Until the late 1980s, blood samples could only be analyzed for nonspecific human blood groups (e.g., ABO blood types). Now, blood and other body fluids and tissues can be analyzed to determine an individual's unique DNA profile.

All forensic scientists examine physical evidence in a series of analysis steps. They first must identify the evidence: Is it a food stain or a bloodstain? Once the evidence is identified—say as a bloodstain—it can be compared to known examples or samples. Is it animal blood or human blood? If it is human blood, is it from a male or female? What is the blood type? Physical evidence is most valuable when an investigator can demonstrate that it is unique—what forensic scientists term individualization. Evidence that is highly individualized can eliminate certain suspects. Many people have the same blood type, but only a single individual has a certain DNA profile (with the exception of identical twins).

DNA and blood analysts often work for crime labs such as those run by the FBI, local law enforcement agencies, universities, and private companies. They prepare and analyze DNA from criminal evidence—such as bloodstains. They interpret the results of their DNA analysis and are often required to testify in court as expert witnesses on their findings.

You will use this book as a guide to learning about blood, bloodstains, and DNA. You will have an opportunity to analyze DNA profiles and bloodstain patterns. Of course, you will not use real blood; you can make fake blood so that you can learn more about the forensic tests.

Tools You Will Need

All forensic investigators carry a case notebook. You should too. It will help you organize facts and record data. Almost all of the materials you will need as a forensic investigator can be obtained around the house or in local stores. Your science teacher can help provide the special chemicals you will need to do some of the forensic tests described in this book.

Keeping Safe As a Junior Forensic Investigator

The most important ingredient for success is safety.

1. Be serious about forensic science. An easygoing attitude can be dangerous to you and to others. Always investigate under the supervision of a knowledgeable adult.

2. Read instructions carefully and completely before beginning with any case in this book. Discuss your procedure with a science teacher or other knowledgeable adult before you start. A flaw in your design could cause an accident.

3. Keep your work area clean and organized. Never eat or drink anything while conducting investigations.

4. Wear protective goggles when working with chemicals or when performing any other experiment that could lead to eye injury.

5. Do not touch chemicals with your bare hands unless instructed to do so. Do not taste chemicals or chemical solutions. Do not inhale vapors or fumes from any chemical or chemical solution.

6. Clean up any chemical spill immediately. If you spill anything on your skin or clothing, rinse it off immediately with plenty of water. Then report what happened to a responsible adult.

7. Keep flammable liquids away from heat sources.
8. Always wash your hands after conducting experiments. Dispose of contaminated waste or articles properly.
9. Be a responsible Web surfer. Explore only genuine topic areas approved by a responsible adult.

How This Book Is Organized

Chapter 1 of this book gave you a true-life example of how a cold case was solved by DNA analysis. Chapter 2 will give you important background information about blood and bloodstain analysis. Chapter 4 covers DNA analysis. You will even learn how to analyze a DNA profile and make a report.

In Chapters 3 and 5, you can read about true crime cases that involved identification through blood and DNA analysis. Each of these cases has a project that will provide you with more forensic skills. It also has some science project ideas to practice and expand on what you have learned. You may decide to use one of these ideas to start your own science fair project.

In Chapter 6, you will put your knowledge of blood and DNA analysis to the test. You will create a series of bloodstains for your friends to analyze. Here, you will get the opportunity to analyze an actual DNA profile and see if you can exclude a suspect(s) from consideration.

Lastly, Chapter 7 gives you the analysis findings, and some outcomes of the cases you are following. Let's get to work!

CHAPTER 2

The Science of Blood Analysis

Blood is one of the most common types of evidence found in forensic investigations. Blood is a relatively thick substance, due to the high amount of solids (blood cells) in it. Although it really can't be perfectly quantified, the average volume of a single blood drop is small—about 0.05 milliliters (mL). That means it would take 20 drops of blood to equal a milliliter. Blood has two parts: a protein-rich liquid, and solids. Blood solids are mostly red and white blood cells. The liquid that is left after blood clots is called serum. Both blood and blood serum are useful in forensic analysis.

The forensic serologist is a scientist who studies blood, body fluids, and tissues. A serologist is trained to:

- collect and preserve bloodstain evidence
- identify the source of a stain—is it really a bloodstain?
- determine whether the bloodstain is animal or human

Bloodstains and Spatters

Blood evidence also includes bloodstain patterns, called spatters. Bloodstain spatters can often "describe" the scene of events to a trained crime scene investigator.

When a drop of blood drips from a person or a weapon (see Figure 1b), physical forces influence both the size of the drop as well as its path. This creates a unique bloodstain pattern that can be studied and analyzed by forensic scientists.

Forensic investigators use chemical tests to identify blood, and bloodstain patterns to describe what happened at the crime scene.

Is It Blood?

At times, a crime scene investigator comes upon an unidentified dry stain. Is it rust, shoe polish, fruit juice, or dried blood? Table 1 lists the methods forensic investigators use to detect bloodstains.

KASTLE-MEYER TEST

Since the early 1900s, the Kastle-Meyer test has been used to quickly test a sample for the presence of blood. The test detects peroxidase, an iron-containing enzyme, and hemoglobin, the iron-containing protein that gives blood its red color. Peroxidase is found in most plant cells and some animal cells; hemoglobin is found in blood cells. So, if this test is positive, it means the sample could be either blood or plant cell material. If the test is negative, you know the sample is *not* blood.

LUMINOL REAGENT TEST

Sometimes a bloodstain is present but it is too faint to be seen by the human eye. Since 1937, forensic investigators have used the chemical luminol to identify

FIGURE 1

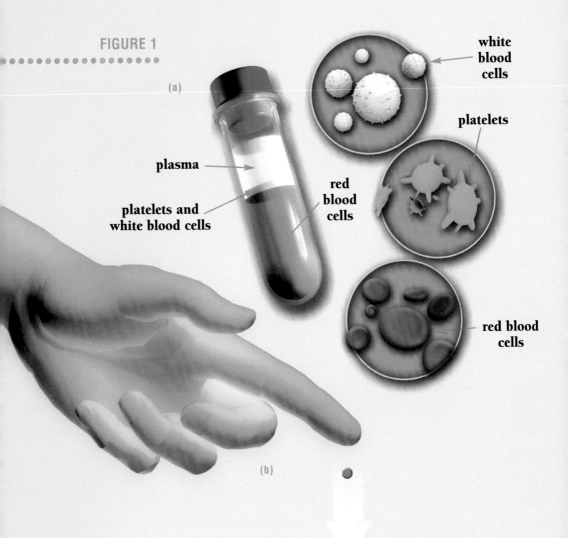

(a) plasma

platelets and white blood cells

white blood cells

platelets

red blood cells

red blood cells

(b)

(a) Blood is a body tissue made of solids within a liquid. In the laboratory, blood in a test tube can be separated into layers. The liquid portion of blood is called plasma. Most of the plasma is water (about 90 percent), the rest is dissolved proteins. The solids are platelets along with red and white blood cells. White blood cells are the only blood cells that have a nucleus, and thus DNA.

(b) When a drop of blood falls from the source, it falls as a round drop. But physical forces affect the size of the drop and the path that it travels. The resulting bloodstain pattern can be studied by forensic scientists.

TABLE 1. Methods for Detecting Bloodstains

DETECTION METHOD	ANALYSIS	
Visual, White Light	Bloodstains will range in color from bright red to brown to dark green.	
Kastle-Meyer Test	A pink/purple color or bubbling shows the presence of blood.	
Luminol Reagent Test	Bloodstains treated with luminol glow blue.	
Human Precipitin Test	A white, cloudy substance is formed when human blood reacts with a special human protein.	

these faint bloodstains. When luminol reagent contacts hemoglobin in blood or peroxidase, the sample glows blue. Although luminol is a very sensitive test, it, like the Kastle-Meyer test, can only suggest that a stain is possibly blood. Its results must be confirmed by other tests.

HUMAN PRECIPITIN TEST

Once a sample is confirmed to be blood, the next step is to find out if it is *human* blood. It is crucial for forensic scientists to know the source of a bloodstain. To find out, scientists perform the precipitin test.

During this procedure, serologists expose samples from a crime scene to a solution. The solution contains proteins that stick to human-specific substances in the crime scene stain. If the sample is human blood, a reaction occurs. The antigens (unique chemical substances) in the crime scene stain and the antibodies (special blood proteins) in the solution form white clumps. Variations of this test can be used to also identify blood as having come from a specific animal.

Identifying Individuals Versus Groups

You have now learned of some tests and analyses that forensic scientists perform on crime scene stains, blood, and bloodstains. These tests can only identify a group (e.g., human or animal), not a specific individual.

For example, one type of blood test a serologist uses can tell to which of the four main human blood groups (type A, B, AB, or O) an individual belongs. The rarest

Forensic science is about *excluding individuals* from a population of possible suspects.

of the human blood groups is blood type AB. In North America, less than 5 percent of individuals are AB blood type. Even though the AB blood group is rare, finding it at a crime scene automatically includes a lot of individuals for consideration. Forensic science is about excluding individuals from a population of possible suspects.

Report to the Court

All forensic scientists must summarize and report their findings (conclusions) to law enforcement authorities and the Court. They present formal pretrial reports and testimony. Your report should be word-processed, typed, or written clearly in blue or black ink.

Your report to the Court should contain the following parts and be in this order:

- Observation of data
- Interpretation of data
- Hypothesis
- Testing of hypothesis and procedures followed
- Summary; findings of fact

In law, "findings" are the conclusions reached by an analysis. In forensic science, findings of fact are scientific conclusions that can be supported by experimental data. Many times, a certain finding—a match in a DNA profile or where an individual was when he was attacked—is only a piece of the puzzle. It is up to the jury, or a judge, to use these facts in deciding a case.

●●●●●●●●●●●●●●●●●●

Inspector's Blood Casebook

The six cases in this chapter are true-life crimes involving blood and bloodstain pattern analyses. You will learn how scientists used forensic techniques to investigate or solve these cases. Then you will use these same detection skills to investigate similar cases of your own.

C A S E   # 1

●●●●●●●●●●●●●●●●

The Case of the Overlooked Stain

OBJECTIVE: Stain Analysis—Is It Blood?

THE ACCUSED: Olivia Riner (1972–   )

THE CASE: On December 2, 1991, a fire raced through a home in Thornwood, New York, killing three-month-old Kristie Fischer. The police arrested Kristie's nanny, Olivia Riner, for arson and murder. At trial, on June 18, 1992, a forensic specialist from the Westchester County Forensic Laboratory testified that a bloodstain was discovered on a doorframe about two weeks after the fire. A Kastle-Meyer test was performed on the stain. This initial test showed that it was blood. But this test could not tell investigators if it was human blood.

Olivia Riner, at her 1992 trial.

Ms. Riner did not have any injuries when she was questioned. So, the defense argued that since Ms. Riner had no injuries right after the fire, someone else must have been in the house and left blood evidence behind. That "someone else" may be the guilty arsonist. Ms. Riner was innocent, they claimed. The prosecution, however, told the jury that a volunteer fireman, Thomas Kelsey, and not "someone else," left the bloodstain.

Unfortunately, the blood sample no longer existed, so it could not be retested to determine if it was human blood or whose blood it was. The defense repeatedly tried to show that no direct forensic evidence linked Ms. Riner to the crime. The defense, instead, suggested that the boyfriend of the infant's half sister had taken part in the crime. The jury found that not enough facts were available for the prosecution to prove its case. On July 7, 1992, the jury acquitted Olivia Riner.

PROJECT:

Is This Stain a Bloodstain?

Learn how to make simulated blood that reacts like real blood.

What You Need:

- polyethylene gloves
- safety glasses
- measuring cup
- distilled water
- 8-oz plastic cup
- tablespoon
- teaspoon
- packet of dry yeast powder (from a grocery store)
- sodium carbonate [Na_2CO_3] (washing soda from a grocery store)
- 4 small paper or plastic cups
- 3 eyedroppers
- red food coloring
- toothpicks
- pencil
- 2 cotton cloth pieces or a handkerchief cut into 2 pieces
- microscope slides
- phenolphthalein, in dropping bottle (from a pool supply store)
- hydrogen peroxide [H_2O_2], 3 percent (from a drug store)
- scissors, cuticle type
- magnifying glass

What You Do:

This simulated blood contains the same natural protein (catalase) that actual blood does. Make this simulated blood just prior to use. Use Figure 2 as a guide.

1. Use a measuring cup to measure 100 mL (about 3 oz) of distilled water into a large plastic cup.

2. Add 1 tablespoon sodium carbonate to the water in the cup. Mix with a spoon until all the chemical dissolves.

3. Add 1/8 teaspoon of dry yeast to a small cup.

4. Use the measuring cup to measure 1 oz (30 mL) of distilled water into the small cup containing the dry yeast. Mix using a toothpick.

5. Use the measuring cup to measure 1 oz (30 mL) of sodium carbonate solution. Pour into a second small cup. Use an eyedropper to add 15 to 20 drops of the yeast mixture to the sodium carbonate solution. Add 5 drops of red food coloring. Mix with a toothpick. Use a pencil to label this mixture "simulated blood."

6. Add some distilled water to a third small cup. Add drops of food coloring. Mix with a toothpick. Label this mixture "stain."

7. Apply the "stain" and the "simulated blood" to two pieces of cloth. Allow the stains to dry. You may want to use a pencil to place a special mark on the cloths that only you know, so you can identify the "stain" and the "simulated blood." Have your

FIGURE 2

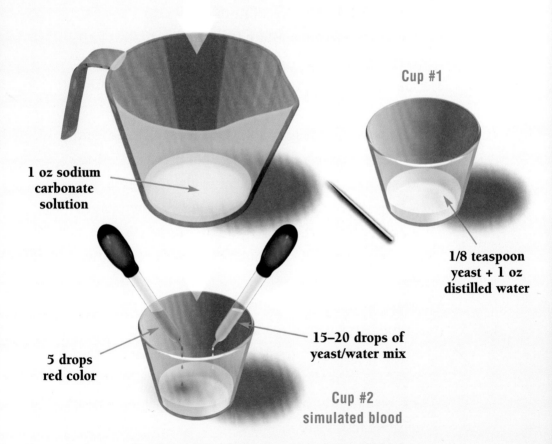

Make sodium carbonate solution.

1 tablespoon sodium carbonate

100 mL (3 oz) distilled water

Cup #1

1 oz sodium carbonate solution

1/8 teaspoon yeast + 1 oz distilled water

5 drops red color

15–20 drops of yeast/water mix

Cup #2 simulated blood

Use this guide to help you make simulated blood.

friends carry out the following Kastle-Meyer test to determine which stain is blood.

Kastle-Meyer Test

SAFETY: Wear safety goggles and polyethylene gloves when carrying out the test. The phenolphthalein solution is flammable; avoid contact with any open flame or hot surface.

1. Pour about 1 oz (30 mL) of 3 percent hydrogen peroxide solution into a fourth small cup.
2. Use scissors to cut a very small piece from the cloth you want to test.
3. Place the small piece of the stained cloth in the center of a clean microscope slide.
4. Use an eyedropper to apply 2 drops of hydrogen peroxide solution to the cloth sample. Wait 20 to 30 seconds. Use a magnifying glass to look for bubbles. Look for small bubbles at first, then larger ones. Bubbles indicate the presence of peroxidase, a positive test result. No bubbles indicate a negative test result.
5. Add a drop of phenolphthalein solution to the cloth sample. Use a toothpick to mix it with the phenolphthalein. A purple/pink color indicates the presence of hemoglobin or peroxidase—a positive test result. Any other color than purple/pink is a negative test result.
6. Repeat Steps 3 to 5 using the other cloth sample.

Science Project Idea

The Kastle-Meyer test can produce false positives—meaning that when the test chemicals are added, a purple/pink color along with foaming results even when the fluid is not blood. The reason is that other peroxidases (plant and animal) are present in the stain. For example, a green vegetable smear may produce a positive test result.

In your notebook create a data table that records peroxidase test results from various natural plant substances: fruit juices, tree saps, and other plant fluids that contain peroxidase and can possibly cause a stain. Apply these substances to pieces of paper towel and allow them to dry. Record which substances show a positive reaction.

See Chapter 7 for a list of substances that give a false positive Kastle-Meyer test result.

C A S E   # 2
●●●●●●●●●●●●●●●●●

The Case of the Stain in Question

THE OBJECTIVE: Determining Whether a Bloodstain Is Human

THE ACCUSED: Boston White; William Lewis

THE CRIME: On Monday morning, September 3, 1883, twenty-three-year-old Rose Ambler was found dead in a field close to her father's house near Stratford, Connecticut. She had been driving there, alone, in a carriage. Marks on her face and neck showed that she had been strangled. There were many heavy footprints in the grass beside her body. There was blood on her clothing. Her fingers were cut and bloody.

Rose Ambler's death needed to be investigated by a public official with responsibility for investigating violent or suspicious deaths—the coroner. Coroner Joyce started assembling the facts of the case.

One suspect was a local farmworker, Boston White. As an ex-convict, White was judged a "shady character" worthy of suspicion. However, Ms. Ambler was recently divorced and was about to marry her ex-husband's cousin, William Lewis. More and more, suspicion turned to Lewis.

Detectives believed that Lewis had changed his mind about marrying Rose, and murdered her. When detectives questioned Lewis they observed bloodstains on his carriage lap robe, a type of blanket worn over a person's lap as he rode in an open carriage. Lewis claimed that the stain was beef blood, and that it was over a year old.

Coroner Joyce asked Dr. Moses White, an expert microscopist, for his help. Dr. White was to investigate if the blood on the lap robe was human blood, and if skin and hair samples taken from Boston White matched the evidence under the victim's bloody fingernails.

Both the precipitin and Kastle-Meyer blood tests (Chapter 2) were not available until decades after Rose Ambler's death. At the Coroner's hearing, Dr. White testified that, based upon microscopic examination, the blanket stains were not blood, but molasses or "some saccharin matter." Dr. White also testified that the skin and hair taken from Boston White did not match the particles found under Ms. Ambler's nails.

The evidence against William Lewis was not con-vincing—the jury decided that he was not a suspect. The murderer was never caught.

PROJECT:
Testing for Human Blood

You will prepare two stains for your friends to test: one "human blood," the other not.

What You Need:

- 3 paper cups
- red and yellow food coloring
- heavy cream
- teaspoon
- 3 eyedroppers
- two 4 x 6-inch pieces of white cotton cloth or handkerchief
- pencil
- water

- vinegar
- measuring cup
- glass microscope slide
- scissors
- black construction paper
- toothpicks
- a friend

You learned about the precipitin test in Chapter 2. Remember, human blood gives a positive precipitin test result because human blood contains special proteins called antigens that react with the antibodies. In fact, all human protein, such as that in saliva, gives a positive result. The simulated blood that you make will give a positive precipitin test when reacting with the simulated antibody solution—vinegar.

What You Do:

1. Add a few drops of yellow food coloring to about 1 oz (30 mL) of water in a paper cup. Add only a single drop of red food coloring. The light yellow color will simulate a serum stain.
2. Measure 1 teaspoon of heavy cream and place it in an empty paper cup.
3. Use a clean eyedropper to add drops of yellow food coloring to the cream until it starts to turn light yellow.
4. Gently pour some of the yellowish water from Step 1 onto the center of a cloth piece. Let it dry, and label it with a pencil "Blood Evidence Sample #1."

5. Gently pour some of the colored cream onto the center of a second cloth piece. Let it dry, and label it with a pencil "Blood Evidence Sample #2."

PERFORMING THE PRECIPITIN TEST

You have been asked to have a colleague (a friend) perform the precipitin test under your direction. The case revolves around pieces of cloth found at the suspect's home. He claims that they are soiled by animal blood. You have prepared the samples for your colleague to analyze using the human precipitin test. Can your friend determine if the stains are human?

1. Use scissors to remove a small piece of stained cloth marked "Blood Evidence Sample #1." Place it on a clean microscope slide.

2. Place the slide with the piece of cloth over a piece of black construction paper.

3. Pour a small amount of vinegar into a paper cup. Use a clean eyedropper to apply 2 to 4 drops of vinegar to the cloth. Use a clean toothpick to move the cloth around in the drops of vinegar. Look for white flakes or particles—this is a sign of a positive precipitin test. Compare this result to the one shown in Table 1.

4. Record the test result in your notebook.

5. Repeat steps 1 through 4 on the bloodstain on the cloth marked "Blood Evidence Sample #2."

What are your friend's findings? See Chapter 7 for an explanation of the findings.

Science Project Idea

Both the precipitin and Kastle-Meyer blood tests involve various blood proteins. Time, heat, and the application of chemicals can break down proteins that can affect test results. **With the help of an adult**, design experiments that test how time, heat, or applying chemicals like detergents, can affect precipitin (Case #2), peroxidase (Case #1), and luminol (Case #7) test results.

CASE #3

●●●●●●●●●●●●●●●●●●●

The Case of the Almost Perfect Murder

OBJECTIVE: Predicting Events From Bloodstain Patterns

THE SCOUNDREL: G. Edward Grammer (1917–1954)

THE CRIME: On August 31, 1952, G. Edward Grammer, the soft-spoken husband of thirty-three-year-old Dorothy Grammer, was charged by Maryland police with her murder. Mrs. Grammer's body was found in the wreck of the family car near Towson, Maryland.

Shortly after midnight on August 20, two police officers observed the family car driving wildly and overturn. The car was not heavily damaged. The two officers rushed to the scene to give aid. They found Dorothy Grammer dead in the car.

Dr. Russell S. Fisher, the Maryland State Medical Examiner, examined the body. He found that Dorothy Grammer had several head gashes and a fractured skull. Careful examination of the bloodstains on her face showed an interesting fact—they ran the wrong way given the car's tipped position. Based on the bloodstain marks and the extent of the injuries, Dr. Fisher reasoned that her injured body had been placed in the car before the crash. The bloodstain evidence was supported by additional evidence. A small stone had been shoved under the heel of the accelerator to force it down.

In his report, Dr. Fisher said that Mrs. Grammer's fractured skull could not have been caused by the crash since the interior damage to the car was slight. Blood-stain evidence showed the body had been in another position than was observed by police at the scene.

On September 11, Edward Grammer was sent to trial for the murder of his wife. At trial, Detective Holmes read from notes taken at the interrogation of Edward Grammer. Holmes testified that Grammer told him that both he and his wife had been arguing in the car. Grammer said that his wife was tired of his late work hours. Further, she claimed, his job was more important than she was. "I stopped to get some gas, and got out of the car. I saw a pipe and hit her once, I remember," Grammer told Holmes. The state charged that Grammer killed his wife because he was hopelessly in love with another woman, Miss Mathilda Mizibrocky.

On October 23, 1952, George Edward Grammer was convicted of murder.

PROJECT:

Creating Bloodstain Patterns

What You Need:

- cornstarch
- water
- tablespoon
- measuring cup
- corn syrup
- dish
- green and red food coloring
- white glue
- teaspoon
- plastic drop cloth
- eyedropper
- pencil
- protractor
- about 40 white construction paper pieces, each 4 inches square
- items to support the squares, such as books
- tape measure
- adult supervision

What You Do:

You will first need to make some fake blood, so that you can then make a reference collection of bloodstain patterns.

PREPARING SIMULATED BLOOD

1. In a measuring cup mix 4 tablespoons of cornstarch thoroughly with 2/3 cup of water. Add 2/3 cup of corn syrup and mix well.

2. Place 3 teaspoons of the mixture in a dish and add 3 to 5 drops of red food coloring. Then add a few drops of green food coloring to reduce the pinkish coloration of the mixture. If the mixture is too light, add one or two drops more of red food coloring. Add an extra drop of green food coloring if the mixture gets too pink again. (Real blood is dark red to reddish brown.)

3. Add white glue, starting with about 1 or 2 teaspoons, to keep the mixture from becoming too transparent—a common fault with fake blood. Use the teaspoon to mix well. Check flowability by stirring and rapidly raising the teaspoon. A good batch of fake blood has a heavy, watery look as it is stirred. Add additional corn syrup or white glue, as needed, to even out the entire effect.

Categories of Bloodstains

There are three categories of bloodstains: passive, transfer, and projected (see Table 2).

MAKING BLOODSTAIN PATTERNS

By looking at bloodstain shapes, you can figure out the angle and height from which the blood fell.

TABLE 2. Bloodstain Categories

BLOODSTAIN CATEGORY

PASSIVE BLOODSTAINS

Bloodstains stains created by the force of gravity acting alone.

Examples: (a) Drops on smooth surface
(b) Drops on rough surface
(c) Dripped pattern

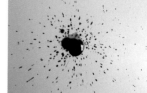

TRANSFER BLOODSTAINS

Bloodstain created when a wet, bloody surface comes into contact with another surface.

Examples: (a) Wipe, smear, or smudge
(b) Contact impressions

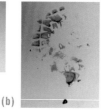

PROJECTED BLOODSTAINS

Bloodstains created when blood is subjected to a force greater than the force of gravity.

Examples:

1. **Cast-off Stains** (Blood released from a blood-bearing object in motion.)

2. **Impact Spatter** (Bloodstain patterns caused when a blood source receives a force that creates smaller drops that scatter in a random pattern.)

   (a) **Low-velocity impact spatter**
   (Large stain 4 mm in size or greater. Force of 5 feet/sec.)

   (b) **Medium-velocity impact spatter**
   (Stain 1 to 4 mm in size. Force of 5 to 25 feet/sec.)

   (c) **High-velocity impact spatter**
   (Stain up to 1 mm in size. Force of 100 feet/sec.)

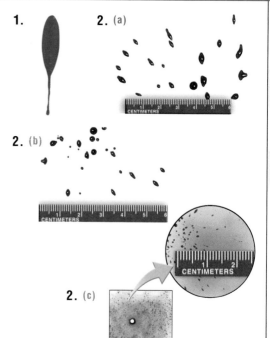

1. Cover your basement, garage, or kitchen floor with a plastic drop cloth. Allow a single drop of simulated blood to form and fall from an eyedropper onto a 4-inch square of white construction paper that sits on the drop cloth. The dropper should be held 6 inches above the paper.

2. Repeat Step 1 from a height of 12 inches, 4 feet, and 7 feet onto separate paper pieces. (**Have an adult drop the simulated blood from a height greater than 4 feet.**) Use a pencil to write the information (drop distance, 90-degree impact angle) on the lower right corner of each cardboard square.

3. Repeat Step 2, this time varying the tilt of the construction paper pieces as well. Use a protractor and some supports to create various impact angles: 80, 70, 60, 50, 40, 30, 20, and 10 degrees. Use Figure 3 as a guide. Allow a single droplet to form and fall over a vertical distance of 6 inches, 12 inches, 4 feet, and 7 feet. Allow the simulated blood droplets to dry.

4. Use a pencil to write the drop test information (impact angle, distance) on the lower right corner of each construction paper piece.

5. Keep the white construction paper pieces as a reference guide for future investigations.

   Based upon your blood drop studies, can you write a general prediction concerning the following questions?

FIGURE 3

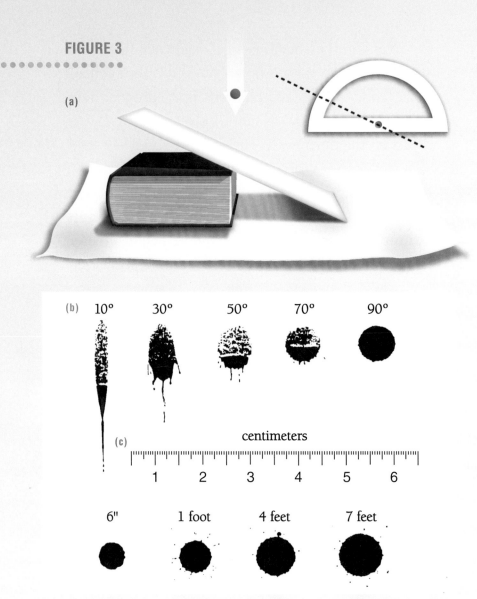

(a)

(b) 10°   30°   50°   70°   90°

(c)   centimeters

1   2   3   4   5   6

6"   1 foot   4 feet   7 feet

(a) By using white cardboard squares and some supports, you can create bloodstain patterns that contact the surface at differing angles. Use a protractor to help you place the cardboard at the correct angles.

(b) The shape of bloodstains changes as the angle of impact changes.

(c) Bloodstain diameters increase as the height from which they fall increases. Eventually, the blood drop reaches a terminal velocity and the size no longer increases.

- Are there differences in drop shape between your results on rough paper surface and those illustrated in Figure 3 on smooth surfaces?
- Do drops made at 90 degrees on a rough surface have a different shape than those on a smooth surface?
- Is there a difference in the diameter of drops made on a rough surface as compared to a smooth surface?
- Do single blood drops break up before they hit a surface? Even from great heights?
- Does the shape of the blood drops striking a rough surface change with the angle of impact?

See Chapter 7 for analysis findings.

TABLE 3. Data for Falling Blood Drops

HEIGHT OF FALL	SPEED BLOOD WAS MOVING	DROP SHAPE
24 inches	2.8 feet/sec	
24 inches	6.3 feet/sec	
24 inches	10 feet/sec	

Science Project Idea

Can you calculate the speed of blood drops? Spread out a roll of brown wrapping paper on the floor, creating a paper "runway." Use a tape measure to measure and mark a distance of 20 feet, in 10-foot increments. Have a friend use a watch to time how long it takes you to walk the measured 20 feet. Dip your finger in a cup of simulated blood. Hold your hand down at you side while at the same time walking normally down the paper runway. Drops of blood will fall from your finger onto the paper surface. Use a pencil to circle all of the drops that fall in the last ten feet (your best walking stride). Number the drops "#1" for the first trial. Do several more trials, walking faster, and running. Make sure that your dipped finger is held down at your side.

After the trial walks and runs, use scissors to cut out a representative set of drops—one for each trial. Paste these into your notebook. Next to each drop calculate how fast you were traveling—the velocity in feet per second. For example, if it took you two seconds to travel ten feet your velocity is 5 feet/second (10 feet ÷ 2 seconds).

When a drop of blood (actually a sphere) strikes a flat surface, the diameter of the sphere in flight will equal the width of the stain on the surface. Compare your blood drop data with that presented in Table 3. Does your data allow you to accurately predict a drop's speed?

• • • • • • • • • • • • • • •

The Case of the Speckled T-shirt

OBJECTIVE: Using Bloodstain Patterns to Tell a Story

THE SCOUNDREL: Chris Jones (1978–   )

THE CRIME: Murder

On February 15, 2000, Chris Jones clocked out from his job at 10:34 P. M. He got into his car and drove to the Buck Island Trailer Park in Tunica County, Mississippi.

At 11:29 P. M., the Sheriff's Department received a 911 call from Jones. Jones told the dispatcher that there was a "possible homicide" at his home. Deputy Woods arrived shortly after. He found Jones standing outside his trailer, crying. Jones was wearing a T-shirt. It had blood on it. So did the upper portion of his jeans and his shoes. Deputy Woods handcuffed Jones and placed him in his patrol car.

Inside the trailer lay Jennifer Stewart. She had a scarf around her neck. Dr. Steven Hayne, a forensic pathologist, later determined that Stewart had been stabbed, and that the wounds were fatal. Deputies gathered crime scene evidence. They photographed various bloodstain patterns, and tagged and preserved physical evidence—including Stewart's scarf and Jones' T-shirt. A deputy removed the T-shirt from Jones and placed it in an evidence bag. No weapon was recovered at the scene.

The physical evidence was sent to the Mississippi crime laboratory. There, forensic scientists began their examination. Christie Smith, a forensic serologist, began by removing the T-shirt from the evidence bag. In a lab notebook, she recorded where the reddish brown bloodstains were located. She then selected representative stains to perform a Kastle-Meyer screening test. This test was positive. She then used scissors to cut out another, similar stain and added the precipitin reagent. The test was positive for human blood.

Grant Graham, a forensic bloodstain examiner, also examined the T-shirt and scarf. He noted in his report that the bloodstain pattern on the T-shirt was consistent with that on the scarf.

At Jones' trial, Graham testified that at sometime the T-shirt had made contact with the scarf. He further testified that certain bloodstains on the T-shirt were consistent with it being close to blood castoffs associated with a stabbing.

A bloodstain expert for the defense countered Graham's bloodstain pattern testimony. Paul Kish testified that the transfer pattern on Jones' T-shirt was a result of Jones moving Stewart's body and placing her on the bed, not from stabbing her.

In April 2004, a jury found Chris Jones guilty of murder. He was sentenced to life in prison.

Determining the Impact Angle of a Blood Drop

When blood hits a surface, a splash pattern will result. These bloodstain patterns can be read by an investigator to help understand what happened at a crime scene. Forensic scientists study bloodstain patterns to locate the point from which the blood that produced the bloodstain originated—the point of origin. To do this they first have to examine individual bloodstains and use them to determine the angle at which they hit the surface. This angle is called the impact angle. Figure 4 shows an illustration of a drop of blood striking the surface at an angle. Look closely at the drop. It has two parts. A large "parent drop" and a smaller "castoff." The tail of the parent drop, and its castoff, points to the direction of travel.

Figure 4e shows a close-up of a drop of blood. Use a metric ruler to measure the length and width of the parent drop in millimeters (mm). Now calculate the width/length ratio by dividing the drop width by drop length. Use this fraction (0.23) to find the impact angle in degrees by using the graph in Figure 5. First, locate the 0.23 W/L value and read the point where it meets the curve—the impact angle. Your answer should be an impact angle of about 12 degrees.

FIGURE 4

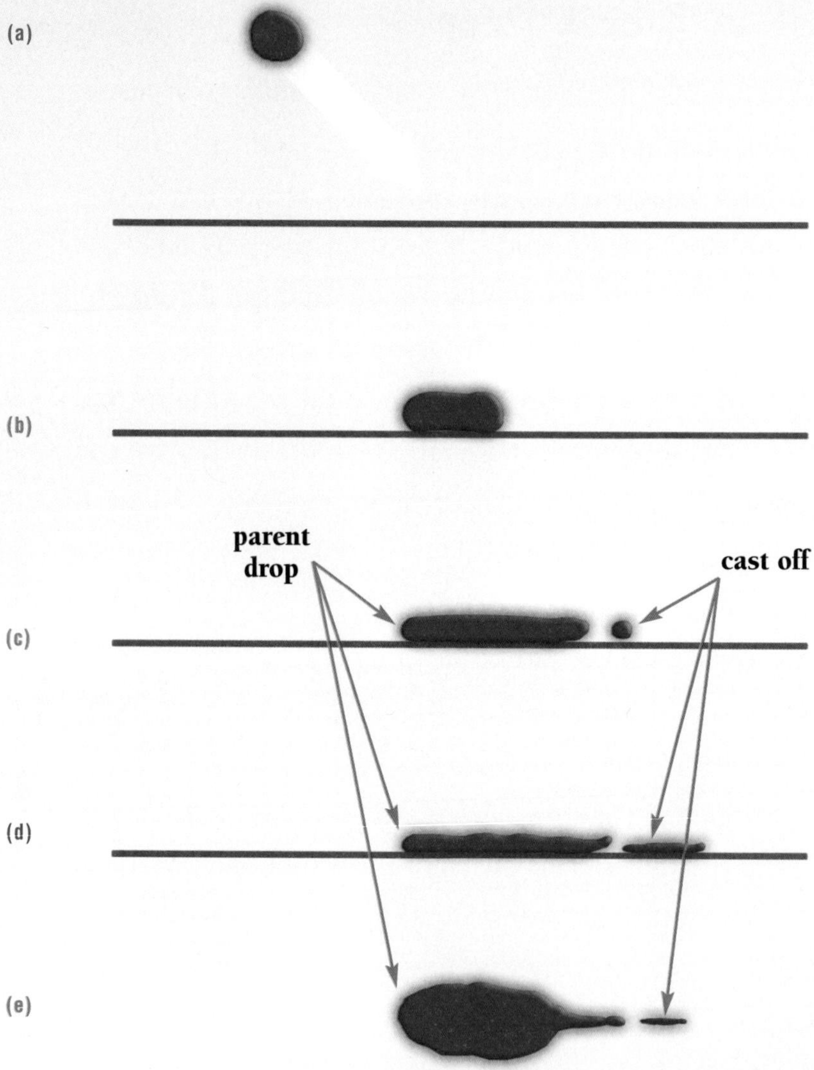

(a)

(b)

parent drop   cast off

(c)

(d)

(e)

(a–d) This side view shows a blood drop traveling toward a surface at an angle of less than 90 degrees. The blood drop strikes the surface, and a tail and castoff form. The tail points in the direction of travel.

(e) This top view of the impact blood drop shows the parent drop, the tail, and the castoff.

PROJECT:

Locating the Point of Origin in a Bloodstain Pattern

What You Need:

- drawing of bloodstain pattern evidence (Figure 6)
- tape
- metric ruler
- pencil
- colored string or yarn
- scissors
- protractor

What You Do:

1. Figure 6 shows a bloodstain pattern. Make a photocopy of it, without enlarging or reducing it. With adult permission, use tape to position this pattern image on a wall—approximately 4 feet above the floor.
2. Copy Table 4 into your notebook.
3. Use a metric ruler to measure the width and length, in millimeters, of each numbered drop. Record these measurements in the notebook table.
4. Use scissors to cut colored string or yarn into ten 4-foot lengths.
5. Tape a piece of string to the center of each blood drop.
6. With some friends to help, hold the string out from the drop using a protractor to display the correct

FIGURE 5

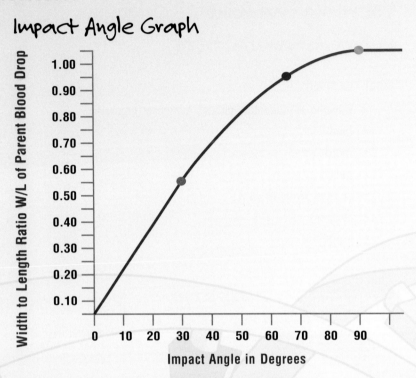

Impact Angle Graph

This graph shows the relationship between an impact angle of a bloodstain (in degrees) and the width-to-length ratio. To find the impact angle of your blood drop for which you have measured the width and length, first find the w/l ratio on the y-axis. Then follow along the x-axis from that point until you intersect the line. From that point on the line, read down to get the corresponding impact angle.

impact angle (Table 4, column 5). Make sure the string travels along the lengthwise axis of each drop.

7. The point in space where all ten drops meet is called the point of origin—the point where each drop of blood began its journey. This point in space links the weapon and the victim—its position and direction of travel.

From what direction did your drops come? Compare your results to those photographed (Figure 14) in Chapter 7.

Science Project Idea

Make sure you have **adult permission** to do this project—even fake bloodstains are not easy to clean up!

Use a pencil as a blunt object. Tape white or brown wrapping paper on a garage floor and wall. Dip your blunt weapon into some simulated blood (Case #1). Try out various striking poses—position(s) and direction(s) that the "weapon" (pencil) takes. While in each pose, swing the pencil, dipped in simulated blood, to create different bloodstain patterns on paper. For example, a downswing of a weapon will leave a different bloodstain pattern than if it was lifted upward or swung from side

FIGURE 6

Wall Bloodstain Pattern

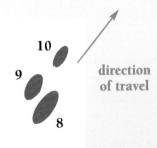

Make a photocopy of this bloodstain pattern. Do not enlarge or reduce the image. Tape the pattern on a wall, approximately four feet above the floor. Can you determine the impact angle and the point of origin for this bloodstain pattern?

TABLE 4. *Analysis Table For Impact Angle Calculations*

DROP NUMBER	WIDTH (mm)	LENGTH (mm)	W/L RATIO	IMPACT ANGLE (From Figure 5)
1				
2				
3				
4				
5				
6				
7				
8				
9				
10				

to side. Remember to use clean sheets of paper for each strike pose and to label the papers. Document the pose with a camera. You may want to construct a number of storylines for each strike pose. Try to devise strike poses that would answer the following questions:

- How does this splash pattern indicate the direction of travel (e.g., up or down; left or right)?
- Which strike movement creates more castoffs—downswings or upswings?
- Is there a relationship between blood drop shape and the distance the drops traveled?

CASE # 5

●●●●●●●●●●●●●●●

The Case of the Telling Trapdoor

OBJECTIVE: Analyzing a Bloodstain Pattern

THE SCOUNDREL: Alfredo Cocchi

THE CRIME: On February 13, 1917, eighteen-year-old Ruth Cruger disappeared. She had told her parents that she was going to Alfredo Cocchi's bicycle shop near 127 Street and Manhattan Avenue in New York to get her ice skates that she had left to be sharpened. Two detectives searched the bicycle shop. Cocchi said that the high school senior had left his shop with her skates. A week

later, Cocchi left the coun-
try—he feared that police
would arrest him even
though he claimed he was
innocent. The police and
District Attorney's office
accepted Cocchi's story.
They had run down
hundreds of leads, but had
not yet found the girl.

Six months after her disappearance, the family hired attorney Grace Humiston to investigate other clues. She turned up a series of spots that appeared to be blood drops on a small, 18-inch-square trapdoor in the back room of Cocchi's bicycle shop. The trapdoor had been recently painted, but the stains still showed through. Humiston called New York Inspector J. J. Kron to the scene. The presence of blood drops was enough evidence to have the trapdoor, and the flooring around it, opened. The police carefully examined the earthen basement floor below. The smooth floor showed evidence of fresh disturbance. The body of Ruth Cruger was found buried in the basement floor. The skates were found buried with her.

Alfredo Cocchi was traced to Bologna, Italy. In the summer of 1917, Cocchi was arrested in Italy. He confessed to the murder, but later said that his wife killed the young girl. A request by New York authorities to bring Cocchi back to the United States was denied. On October 29, 1920, he was convicted in an Italian court and sentenced to 27 years for the murder of Ruth Cruger.

PROJECT:
Analyzing Blood Stain Patterns

You are a bloodstain expert. Detectives investigating a missing person's report have called you to the scene. While interviewing the husband of the missing woman, detectives noticed blood on the kitchen floor tiles (Figure 7). The husband told the detectives that he had recently injured himself with a box cutter while opening a package. The husband is left-handed. His right hand bears the evidence of a deep cut. You are to determine if the bloodstains shown in the detective's illustration in Figure 7 have been thrown from a bloody weapon or are simply drips of blood from his hand. Are there other tests that you could do that would provide additional facts in this case?

What You Need:

- **photocopy of Figure 7**
- **magnifying glass**
- **ruler**

What You Do:

1. Make a photocopy of Figure 7.
2. Use a magnifying glass to examine the numbered blood drops.
3. Use a ruler to measure the diameter of each drop.
4. Make a data table in your notebook that lists the blood drop reference number and its measured diameter in millimeters (mm).
5. Use the blood drop reference card guides you made in Case #3 to help you determine the height from which they fell.
6. Your findings should be summarized in a report. You should include the following:
   - The total volume of blood found on the tile floor.
   - The height from which the drops fell.
   - Does this physical evidence agree with the husband's statement?

FIGURE 7

Bloodstain Pattern on Floor Tile

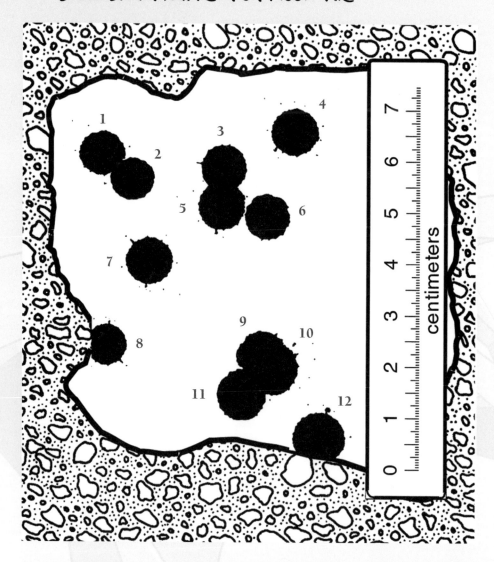

Use this bloodstain pattern to determine the approximate volume of the blood drops and the height from which they fell. Does this evidence agree with the husband's statement?

■ Are there any other tests on the blood drops that
could be done to provide additional findings?

See Chapter 7 for analysis findings.

Science Project Idea

Investigate what shape(s) blood droplets take when
cast off from a weapon swung in an arc. **With adult
permission**, tape brown wrapping paper to the ceiling,
wall, and floor of a room (see Figure 8). Dip a pencil into
some simulated blood. Holding the pencil, extend your
hand behind you, and bring it upward, over your head,
and down to your feet in an arc. **With an adult's help**,
use a stepladder to examine individual drops made at
various angles. Can you tell the position of the object in
space from the shape (circular to oval) of a spatter
droplet? See Chapter 7 for an analysis.

FIGURE 8

Bloodstain Pattern on Floor Tile

With adult permission, attach a roll of brown paper to the ceiling, walls, and floor of a room. Then swing a pencil, dipped in simulated blood, to create blood spatter evidence on the brown paper.

CASE #6

The Case of the Glowing Light

OBJECTIVE: Detecting Trace Amounts of Blood

THE SCOUNDRELS: Pauline and Walter John Zile

THE CRIME: Murder

On October 22, 1994, twenty-four-year-old Pauline Zile contacted the Broward County Sheriff's office. She told investigators that her daughter, Christina, had been abducted from a ladies' room while the two were at a flea market west of Fort Lauderdale, Florida. Deputies, afraid that a kidnapping had taken place, contacted the FBI. Christina's case even aired on the TV series *America's Most Wanted*.

On October 27, detective Robert Foley received Pauline's permission to search their apartment in the hope of finding additional clues. There, Foley discovered drops of blood on a pillow, mattress, and box spring in the girl's bedroom. He sprayed a chemical, luminol, on the bed frame, headboard, mattress, and the surrounding walls. He observed a blue, luminous glow indicating the possible presence of blood. He also sprayed the couch and rugs in the living room. Foley took samples of the victim's clothing that appeared to be stained for detailed analysis.

Walter John Zile at his trial

Later, sheriff's investigators confronted Pauline Zile with the evidence of blood in her apartment. Christina had not been abducted. It appeared that she had been assaulted. Confronted by the evidence, Pauline told investigators that her husband was the one who had assaulted Christina. Questioned later by deputies, Walter John Zile confessed to assaulting the girl. He said he was trying to prevent her from crying when she went into convulsions and died. He later agreed to take investigators to where he had buried the body.

Both Pauline and Walter Zile were convicted of aggravated child abuse and murder.

PROJECT:

Detecting Trace Amounts of Blood

What You Need:

- an adult
- safety glasses
- dishwashing gloves
- 10 soda bottle screw caps
- sheet of paper

54

- pencil
- paper cup marked "water"
- paper cup marked "waste water"
- distilled or bottled water
- red food coloring
- household bleach
- toothpicks
- 2 eyedroppers
- funnel
- spray bottle
- luminol (from your science teacher)
- teaspoon
- sodium carbonate [Na_2CO_3] (washing soda from a grocery store)
- measuring cup
- hydrogen peroxide [H_2O_2], 3 percent (from a drug store)
- ten 4-inch-square pieces of cotton cloth or handkerchiefs
- old table
- plastic drop cloth
- dark room

Luminol and Blood

Luminol can detect very small amounts of blood—as little as a single drop of blood in a million drops of water, or 1 part blood in 1,000,000 parts water. The luminol reacts with the iron in blood to produce a bluish glow. It can also react with other substances, including chlorine bleach. Naturally we cannot use actual human or animal blood in our investigation. Instead, you will make simulated blood using chlorine bleach as a substitute for blood hemoglobin. Then you will dilute the simulated blood to a point where it cannot be seen, but still can be detected. The purpose of the investigation is to learn just how sensitive luminol is in detecting evidence of a simulated bloodstain.

What You Do:

SAFETY: **Wear safety glasses and dishwashing gloves when working with chemical reagents. Always have an adult present.**

PREPARING SAMPLE BLOODSTAINS

Use Table 5 and Figure 9 as guides when doing these steps.

1. On a table, arrange 10 soda bottle screw caps (cleaned and thoroughly rinsed with distilled water). Line them up on a sheet of paper. Use a pencil to number nine caps from 1 to 9. Place two cups, labeled "water" and "waste water," near the paper sheet. Fill both cups halfway with distilled water.

2. In the tenth cap, combine 5 drops of red food coloring with 5 drops of household bleach. Mix using a clean toothpick. This mixture is the simulated blood sample.

3. You will be performing a stepwise dilution of the simulated blood sample. You will use distilled water to dilute (to lower or wash away) the concentration of the blood. Use a clean eyedropper to add 9 drops of water to cap 1. Then add one drop of simulated blood from cap 10. Mix with a clean toothpick. Take the remaining simulated blood in

56

FIGURE 9

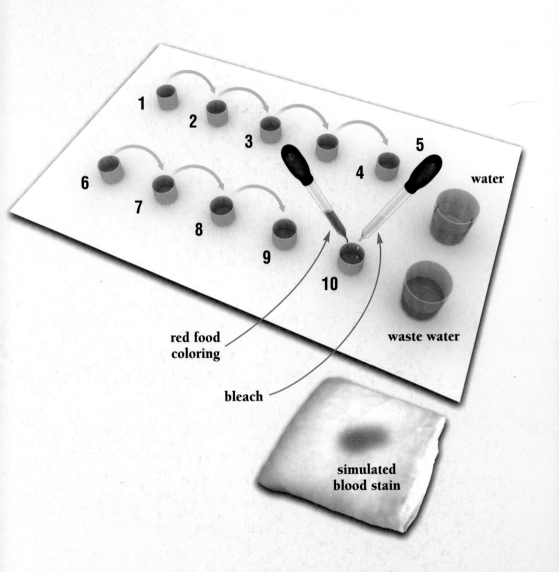

Using soda bottle caps, water, and simulated blood, you can study how the concentration of "blood" affects the luminol test.

cap 10 and "spill" it onto the center of a clean 4-inch cloth square. On the outside edge of the cloth, mark "simulated blood." Rinse out the eyedropper in the cup of "waste water." The concentration (amount of blood in the water) in cap 1 is one part blood per ten parts solution. See Table 5.

4. Add 9 drops of water to cap 2. Transfer one drop of the diluted (weaker) "blood" from cap 1 to cap 2. Mix with a clean toothpick. Now the concentration of "blood" in cap 2 is 1/10 x 1/10, which equals 1/100. Take the remaining simulated blood in cap 1 and "spill" it onto the center of a clean 4-inch cloth square. On outside edge of the cloth, mark it "simulated blood—1/10." Rinse out the eyedropper in the cup of "waste water."

5. Repeat step 4 for the remaining caps—3 through 9. For example, add 9 drops of water to cap 3 and transfer 1 drop from cap 2 to cap 3; mix. Take the remaining simulated blood in cap 2 and spill it onto the center of a clean 4-inch cloth square. Mark this cloth "simulated blood—1/100."

6. In your notebook, make a table (see Table 5) in which you can record your luminol test results. In the table, list the decreasing simulated blood concentration in one column. Add a fourth column to record whether a reaction happened (a bluish glow). Add a fifth column to record any other

TABLE 5. *Analysis Table for Determining the Sensitivity of the Luminol Reagent*

CAP	DILUTION	CONCENTRATION OF SIMULATED BLOOD	REACTION TO LUMINOL REAGENT (yes / no)	COLOR ON CLOTH (yes / no)
10	0	—		
1	1/10 drops	1/10		
2	1/10 x 1/10 drops	1/100		
3	1/10 x 1/10 x 1/10 x drops	1/1,000		
4	1/10 x 1/10 x 1/10 x 1/10 drops	1/10,000		
5	1/10 x 1/10 x 1/10 x 1/10 x 1/10 drops	1/100,000		
6	1/10 x 1/10 x 1/10 x 1/10 x 1/10 x 1/10 drops	1/1,000,000		
7	1/10 x 1/10 x 1/10 x 1/10 x 1/10 x 1/10 x 1/10 drops	1/10,000,000		
8	1/10 x 1/10 x 1/10 x 1/10 x 1/10 x 1/10 x 1/10 x 1/10 drops	1/100,000,000		
9	1/10 x 1/10 x 1/10 x 1/10 x 1/10 x 1/10 x 1/10 x 1/10 x 1/10 drops	1/1,000,000,000		

observations such as if a red color could be seen on the cloth.

MAKING THE LUMINOL TEST SOLUTION

(Make this solution prior to use.)

1. Cover an old table with a protective plastic drop cloth. Spread out each of the ten 4-inch-square cloth pieces on the drop cloth.

2. Place a kitchen funnel onto a spray bottle with the spray head removed.

3. **Under adult supervision**, measure 0.3 grams (⅛ teaspoon) of luminol. Dump the measured luminol into the funnel. (You will flush it, and other chemicals, down into the bottle in a later step.)

4. Measure 13 grams (2 tablespoons) of sodium carbonate. Dump this measured amount into the funnel.

5. Measure 250 mL (1 cup) of distilled water. Pour it into the funnel to dissolve the solid chemicals.

6. Measure 250 mL (1 cup) of 3 percent hydrogen peroxide solution. Pour it into the funnel to dissolve the solid chemicals. Remove the funnel. Replace the spray head. Carefully shake the bottle to mix the chemicals. Allow the solids to settle and avoid spraying any of these undissolved chemicals. The solution must be used within twenty minutes.

THE LUMINOL TEST

(Perform this test in a darkened room.)

1. Turn off the lights.

2. Spray the luminol solution onto the center of each cloth.

3. After a couple of seconds, look for a bluish glow (see Table 1, p. 16) that tells you that a reaction has occurred and "blood" is present.

4. Record the following data in your notebook:

   ▪ the concentration at which the red color on the cloth disappears.

   ▪ the lowest concentration that the luminol test records a positive result (e.g., presence of "blood").

Forensic scientists believe that the luminol reagent can detect a bloodstain having a hemoglobin concentration of 1/20,000,000. Do your results using a simulated blood (with chlorine atoms instead of hemoglobin) show similar sensitivity?

See Chapter 7 for analysis findings.

Science Project Idea

With adult help, design an experiment to test whether the luminol test is more sensitive than the Kastle-Meyer test for blood. You may want to make the simulated blood used in the peroxidase test (Case #1). Dilute and test this simulated blood like you did in the steps outlined in Table 5.

• • • • • • • • • • • • • • • • • • •

The Science of DNA Analysis

Since 1987, the science of DNA profiling has allowed forensic scientists to exclude or include individuals from a group of suspects. Forensic science can now identify individuals from blood, body fluid, and tissue evidence. Let's learn how.

What Is DNA?

There may be no chemical as important as DNA—deoxyribonucleic acid. It is located in nearly every cell in a person's body. DNA has a set of chemical instructions. These instructions control all of a cell's activities. DNA also carries information that makes every person different.

In the 1950s, Rosalind Franklin (1920–1958), James Watson (1928–   ), Francis Crick (1916–2004), and other scientists studied the DNA molecule. A model of the DNA molecule showed that DNA is made of subunits called nucleotides. The nucleotides are linked together in such a way that the DNA molecule resembles a long, twisted ladder. The rungs of the ladder are made of pairs of nucleotide bases (base pairs) that are bonded

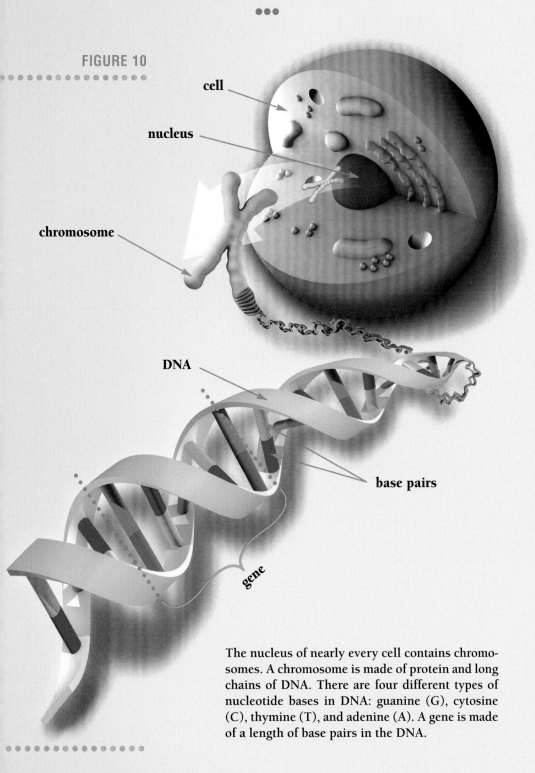

FIGURE 10

cell

nucleus

chromosome

DNA

base pairs

gene

The nucleus of nearly every cell contains chromosomes. A chromosome is made of protein and long chains of DNA. There are four different types of nucleotide bases in DNA: guanine (G), cytosine (C), thymine (T), and adenine (A). A gene is made of a length of base pairs in the DNA.

together (see Figure 10). The nucleotide bases are represented by the letters G, T, A, and C.

DNA and You

Each of us has about 6 billion (3 billon pairs of) nucleotide bases that make up our genetic code, or genome. For example, part of that sequence could be:

G-G-T-A-A-C-T-C-A-G-C-T-C-C-G-G-C-C-G-T-T-
A-A-A-A-T-T-C-G-C-G-C-G

Almost all (99.9 percent) of the genetic code is identical in all humans. The remaining 0.1 percent, or 3 million base pairs, of the genome are different for each of us (except identical twins). These are the parts of the genome used for DNA profiling.

Sections of DNA give instructions for the cell to make proteins. A piece of DNA that contains all of the information needed to build one protein is called a *gene*. A *locus* is a location on the chromosome where alleles are found. (*Loci* is the plural for locus.) All of us have two *alleles* for a particular gene. We get one allele from each parent. These inherited regions of our DNA can vary from person. How do they vary? Let's take a look at an example for D13S317, a locus on chromosome #13.

D13S317 has nine most common forms of the TATC repeat sequence. A person will most likely have two of the following alleles:

1. seven repeating units of TATC—recorded as "7" (i.e., TATCTATCTATCTATCTATCTATCTATC)

FIGURE 11

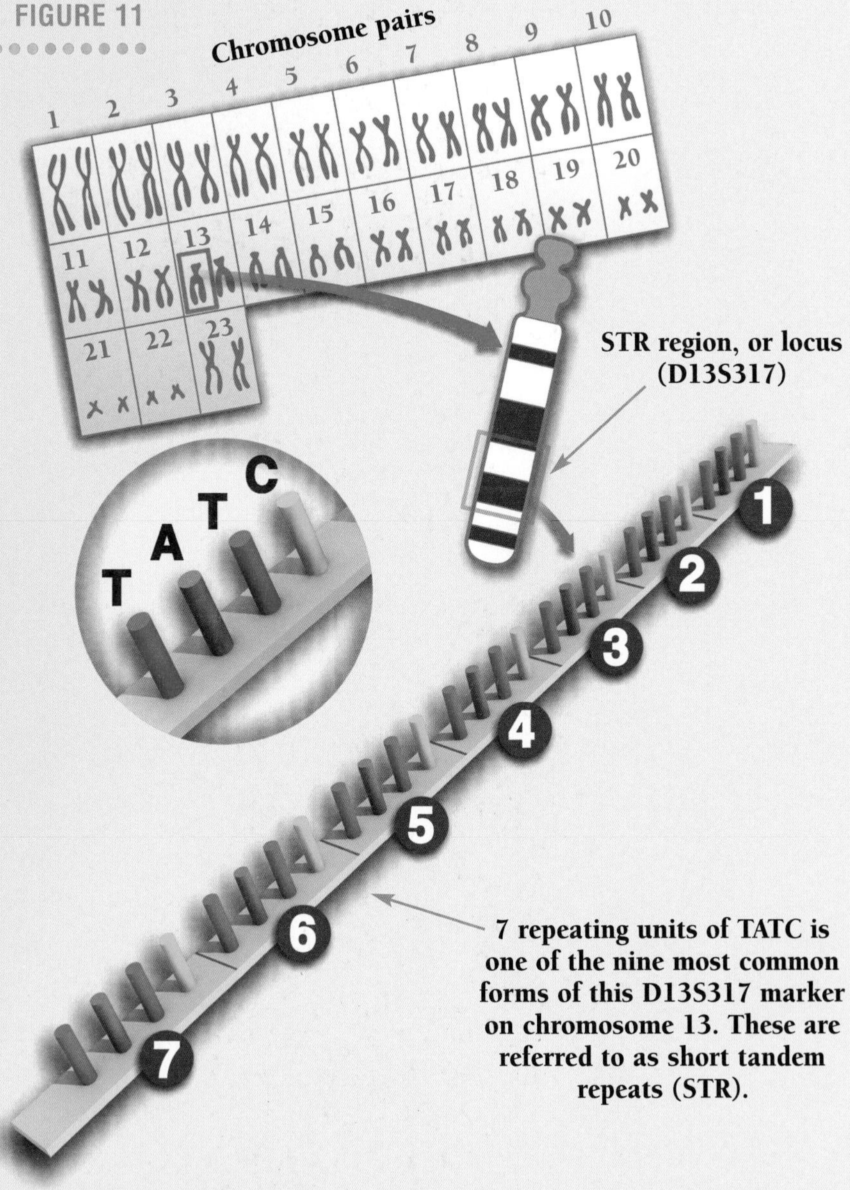

STR region, or locus
(D13S317)

7 repeating units of TATC is one of the nine most common forms of this D13S317 marker on chromosome 13. These are referred to as short tandem repeats (STR).

Humans have 23 chromosome pairs, for a total of 46 chromosomes. One of the CODIS DNA markers on chromosome pair 13 is named D13S317. It is located on chromosome 13 and has at least nine possible alleles of the base sequence TATC. The nine most common forms, or alleles, of the TATC repeating unit are 7, 8, 9, 10, 11, 12, 13, 14, or 15 repeats. All people have two of these D13S317 alleles.

2. eight repeating units of TATC—recorded as "8" (i.e., TATCTATCTATCTATCTATCTATC TATCTATC)

3. nine repeating units of TATC—recorded as "9" (i.e., TATCTATCTATCTATCTATCTATC TATCTATCTATC)

4. ten repeating units of TATC—recorded as "10" (i.e., TATCTATCTATCTATCTATCTATC TATCTATCTATCTATC)

5. eleven repeating units of TATC—recorded as "11" (i.e., TATCTATCTATCTATCTATCTATC TATCTATCTATCTATCTATC)

6. twelve repeating units of TATC—recorded as "12" (i.e., TATCTATCTATCTATCTATCTATC TATCTATCTATCTATCTATCTATC)

7. thirteen repeating units of TATC—recorded as "13" (i.e., TATCTATCTATCTATCTATCTATC TATCTATCTATCTATCTATCTATCTATC)

8. fourteen repeating units of TATC—recorded as "14" (i.e., TATCTATCTATCTATCTATCTATC TATCTATCTATCTATCTATCTATC TATCTATC)

9. fifteen repeating units of TATC—recorded as "15" (i.e., TATCTATCTATCTATCTATCTATC TATCTATCTATCTATCTATCTATC TATCTATCTATC)

For example, one individual could have one allele with nine repeat units and one allele with thirteen repeat units (stated as 9, 13) of the TATC repeat sequence. That means they have nine repeating units at one allele and thirteen repeating units at the other allele for this D13S317 marker. Another person could have seven copies and seven copies (7,7) of the TATC repeat sequence.

DNA and Forensics

Forensic scientists can recover DNA for analysis from body fluids, tissues, hair, bones, and teeth.

In 1997, the FBI announced the selection of thirteen chromosome loci to form a national DNA database called the Combined DNA Index System—CODIS. All public forensic laboratories in the United States that use the CODIS system can enter DNA profiles via computer into the national database.

The odds of finding another human with your exact DNA profile is estimated to be 1 in 1.7 million billion—

250,000 times more than the total human population.

Forensic scientists look at the probability of occurrence of each genotype for all thirteen CODIS markers. This combination of genotypes is called a *DNA profile*—a set of ten to thirteen CODIS marker genotypes.

Forensic scientists perform STR analysis to create a DNA profile. In STR analysis, the DNA left as evidence is compared with a suspect's DNA. When the allele numbers match, forensic scientists call it a DNA match. For example, the odds of finding another human with your exact DNA profile (all thirteen CODIS markers) is estimated to be *1 in 1.7 million billion*—250,000 times more than the total human population.

Steps in STR Analysis

1. DNA COLLECTION

At the crime scene, the main responsibility of crime scene technicians is to collect cells from a number of sources: blood, body fluids (e.g., saliva), and body tissues (e.g., skin cells under fingernails). Cells in these tissues contain DNA. Technicians must be careful not to contaminate any of the samples with DNA from themselves or others.

2. DNA EXTRACTION

In the laboratory, collected cells are broken up, releasing DNA from a cell's nucleus. The DNA is then purified and isolated in solution.

3. DNA AMPLIFICATION

Usually, the amount of collected DNA is too small to analyze right away. It needs to be increased in amount (amplified). This is done through a special process called PCR—polymerase chain reaction. Precise copies of existing DNA are made to increase the count.

4. ANALYSIS

The amplified DNA base sequences are analyzed using the STR analysis method. During amplification, DNA samples are mixed with fluorescent dyes. The DNA samples are then processed in a special gel material. A computer uses a laser to look at specific areas of DNA that were amplified. The resulting computer analysis shows the number of bases for a particular CODIS marker. Figure 12 shows a typical analysis for 5 different individuals using three DNA markers along with a gender (male or female) marker.

Let's take a closer look at Figure 12. Figure 12a shows the three loci used in this particular STR analysis. They are locus D3S1358 on chromosome #3, locus vWA on chromosome #12, and locus FGA on chromosome #4. Remember, in a real DNA analysis, scientists look at ten to thirteen DNA markers. Figure 12b is a reference standard. The first group of peaks are the eight most common forms of the D3S1358 locus for chromosome #3. The second group of peaks are the eleven most common forms of the vWA locus for chromosome #12. The third group of peaks are the

FIGURE 12

STR Analysis of Five Individuals

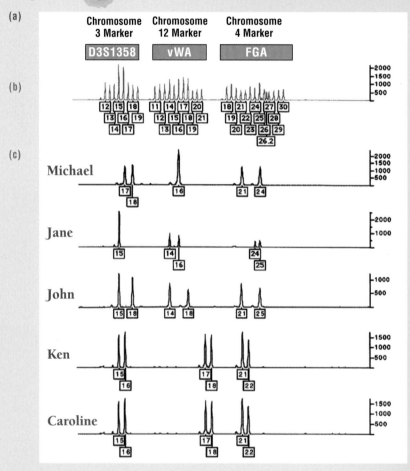

This figure shows an STR analysis for five different people.

(a) The three chromosome markers for this test were marker D3S1358 on chromosome #3; marker vWA on chromosome #12; and marker FGA on chromosome #4.

(b) This reference shows the most common forms of the three markers. This reference is then compared to the samples in (c).

(c) The five people's DNA is also analyzed using STR. Jane has allele 15 (meaning she inherited a 15 marker from her mother and a 15 marker from her father) for the chromosome #3 marker; she has 14 and 16 for chromosome #12 marker; and she has alleles 24 and 25 for chromosome #4 marker.

fourteen most common forms of the FGA locus for chromosome #4. These are the reference peaks that the samples from the five people (12c) are compared to.

DNA from five people (Michael, Jane, John, Ken, and Caroline) was analyzed to see which forms of the repeat units (alleles) they have. The results are shown in Figure 12c. Look at the first set of peaks for each person (for chromosome #3). You will see that Michael has 17 and 18 repeat units of D3S1358, Jane has 15, John has 15 and 18, Ken has 15 and 16, and Caroline has 15 and 16.

If there was DNA evidence from a crime scene, this DNA would also be analyzed during this same STR analysis. Then the DNA results from the evidence could be compared to the DNA results for each person. For example, if the evidence had DNA on it that showed 15 and 18 repeat units at D3S1358, then John is the only person with DNA that matches for that chromosome marker. The chance of getting a random match among unrelated individuals using ten markers is about 1 in 10 billion.

Table 6 is a results table from an STR analysis. Let's learn how to interpret these results.

- Look at the pair of numbers for each person, for each different marker. For example, Suspect 3 has a genotype (pair of numbers) for marker D3 of 17, 17. If you look at the genotypes for the blood on the knife for marker D3, you see the knife and the clothing both have 14, 15, and 16.

TABLE 6. DNA Evidence Profiles (STR Analysis)

Sample	Marking (Sample number)	Allele results for nine chromosome markers, along with gender									
		D3	Gender	D8	D21	D18	D5	D13	D7	FGA	vWA
Suspect #1	S-1	16/16	Male XY	8/11	26/26	18/14	7/16	7/7	7/9	12/16	15/15
Suspect #2	S-2	12/19	Female XX	13/14	26/26	15/16	9/10	8/9	8/9	22/26	15/15
Suspect #3	S-3	17/17	Male XY	8/8	35.2/36	27/27	7/8	7/7	7/8	16/30.2	21/21
Victim	V	14/15	Male XY	10/14	26/31	11/14.2	12/12	8/13	7/7	30/30	15/19
Knife	M-1	14/15/16	XY	8/10/11/14	26/31	11/14/ 14.2/18	7/12/16	7/8/13	7/9	12/16/30	15/19
Bloody Clothing	M-2	14/15/16	XY	8/10/11/14	26/31	11/14/ 14.2/18	7/12/16	7/8/13	7/9	12/16/30	15/19

Most of the time, only two alleles would be present if the stain is from a single source. In this case there are 3 alleles. This indicates that the stain is a mixture of DNA from at least two people. So Suspect 3 does not match for this marker. But suspect 3 does match the evidence for marker D8 (8 matches the 8 on the knife and the clothing). In total, suspect 3 has only two marker matches with the knife and clothing. More importantly suspect 3 doesn't match at D3, D21, D18, D5, D7, FGA, and vWA, so he is excluded as a possible source of the DNA on the knife and clothing.

- Suspect #2 has two matches with the knife and bloody clothing. But suspect #2 can be eliminated because suspect #2 does not match at D3, D8, D18, D5, D13, D7, and FGA on the knife or bloody clothing evidence.
- Suspect #1 has matches to all nine markers. Male blood was found on both the knife and the clothing.
- Both Suspect #1 and the victim's blood are found on both the knife and the clothing evidence.

CHAPTER 5

Inspector's DNA Casebook

The case in this chapter is special because it shows how a new technology came into being with the power to discriminate between individuals in a population. You will learn how scientists use the technology of DNA profiling to eliminate a person or include them in consideration in a forensic case. Then you will use these same detection skills to investigate similar cases of your own.

CASE #7

The Case of the False Conviction

OBJECTIVE: Using a DNA Profile to Prove Innocence

THE ACCUSED: Robert Clark (1960–)

THE CASE: Wrongful Conviction
Peter Neufeld, co-founder of the Innocence Project at Cardozo Law School, a program to free innocent people in prison, decided to get involved in a twenty-four-year-old case.

On July 30, 1981, a man with a gun abducted a woman from a parking lot in East Atlanta, Georgia. They drove away in her car. Later she was robbed and assaulted. The man drove away in her car. The woman contacted authorities and the investigation began.

A couple of days later, the woman spotted her car at various locations in Atlanta. She contacted police who located and impounded it. During the course of their investigations, the Atlanta police determined that Robert Clark was the driver. They contacted him by phone. He agreed to meet with them, but failed to show up. Police later arrested Clark for motor vehicle theft. He became the primary suspect in the assault and robbery case after he was untruthful in how he had obtained the car. His mistake was in trying to protect a friend—Tony Arnold. Instead of telling police that Arnold had lent him the car, he told them that another woman had.

The victim identified Clark as the perpetrator in a lineup. Clark was tried and convicted on May 26, 1982. At the trial, the victim testified that there was no doubt that Clark was the individual who robbed and assaulted her.

There was not enough evidence for investigators to obtain blood typing information. The defense produced an eyewitness who testified that she saw Tony Arnold driving a car similar to the victim's car. The prosecution admitted at the trial that the police did not investigate Tony Arnold after being told by Clark that it was he who lent him the victim's car.

Throughout his incarceration, Robert Clark maintained that he was not guilty. In 2003, the Innocence Project began its independent investigation. In 2005, the case evidence was sent to a DNA testing laboratory. The DNA STR profile identified Tony Arnold, not Robert Clark, as the perpetrator.

On December 8, 2005, Robert Clark was released from prison.

Robert Clark, left, celebrates his new freedom with his son as he leaves court. New DNA evidence showed that Clark was wrongfully convicted of assault and robbery. He spent over twenty-three years in prison for a crime he did not commit.

PROJECT:

Excluding Suspects Using STR DNA Analysis

Police respond to a homicide. The body of an elderly man, William Fletcher, has been discovered in the back room of his goldsmith shop by his daughter. It appears that the motive was robbery.

Fingerprint evidence has provided useful information. The victim's fingerprints were found on an awl (a small, pointed tool). There was one other useful match—it was recovered on the handle of the front doorknob. Investigators have run the print through the FBI's AFIS (Automated Fingerprint Identification System) database. It is a match to Jason Roberts, who has a criminal record.

Investigators have also recovered blood evidence from articles at the crime scene: a large cloth bandana, the awl, and a wooden mallet. The mallet was believed to be the murder weapon. The evidence has been tagged and transported back to the crime lab for analysis.

Witnesses reported no unusual activity near the shop. The victim's daughter has given police the names of two previous employees. One, Henry Treadwell, had left on unfriendly terms. Police begin routine interviews.

Police were not satisfied with Henry Treadwell's alibi (his claim of where he was when the crime occurred). The first thing investigators noticed was a hand injury. Treadwell told police that he had never left the house. The hand injury occurred while he was sharpening an axe to chop wood.

Police also interviewed the other employee, Helen Alderson. The wooden mallet had her fingerprint on it as well. Helen told investigators that she had not been in the shop since she left about five weeks earlier. She agreed to provide investigators with a DNA sample.

Investigators had enough evidence to get two court-ordered warrants for DNA samples. Investigators used cotton swabs to collect cheek cells from Roberts and Treadwell. The samples have been processed using nine DNA markers. DNA profile data has been generated. It is up to you to evaluate the data and write a report that can either eliminate or connect either suspect to the crime scene.

What You Need:

- **Table 7: DNA evidence profiles (STR analysis)**
- **notebook**

TABLE 7. DNA Evidence Profiles (STR Analysis)

Sample	Marking (Sample number)	Gender	DNA Markers								
			D3	D8	D21	D18	D5	D13	D7	FGA	vWA
Roberts	S-1	Male XY	17/17	8/11	35/35	9/27	7/16	7/7	7/9	12/16	17/21
Treadwell	S-2	Male XY	12/19	13/14	26/26	15/16	9/10	8/9	8/9	22/26	15/15
Alderson	S-3	Female XX	17/18	8/8	35.2/36	27/27	7/8	7/7	7/8	16/30.2	21/21
Victim (William Fletcher)	V	Male XY	16/16	10/14	26/31	11/14	12/13	8/13	7/7	30/30	15/19
Cloth	M-1	Male XY	12/19	13/14	26	15/16	9/10	8/9	8/9	22/26	15
Wood Mallet	M-2	Male XY	12/16/19	10/13/14	26/31	11/14/ 15/16	9/10/ 12/13	8/9/13	7/8/9	22/26/30	15/19
Awl	M-3	Male XY	12/19	13/14	26	15/16	9/10	8/9	8/9	22/26	15
Coat	M-4	Male XY	16	10/14	26/31	11/14	12/13	8/13	7	30	15/19

What You Do:

1. Look closely at the data table. For example, in the column for the D3 chromosome marker, compare the alleles found for each of the four people (Roberts, Treadwell, Alderson, and Fletcher) as well as the alleles found on the cloth, mallet, awl, and coat. Which ones match?

See if you can answer these questions:

- Can any of the suspects, Treadwell, Roberts, or Alderson, be eliminated? Why?
- Can the awl be linked to the crime?
- Can the murder weapon be linked to any suspect? The victim?
- Is there any co-mingling of bloodstains? On which article(s)?

See Chapter 7 for analysis findings.

Investigating the Crime

This chapter introduces a "crime" that is based on an actual event. Your friends can solve the crime using the information and cases presented in this book. You will review DNA and blood evidence and advise the court on the findings of fact in the case. Chapter 7 has the analysis findings. As in most forensic cases, this one is not as simple as it appears!

The Case of the Second Examination

THE PROFILE: Steve Hobart is appealing his fifteen-year sentence for assault. He is petitioning the court for a new trial. Among many reasons given, he states that the blood and DNA evidence were incorrectly examined. He wants the court to order a second forensic examination of the following physical evidence:

- a cloth with a stain
- stain on knife blade
- DNA profile

Hobart believes that his ex-girlfriend Marilyn Jones set him up. He told police that he believed that she actually stabbed herself. She told the police that he assaulted her on April 23, 1998. In his appeal for a new trial, Hobart states that the cloth police recovered at his home had a barbeque sauce stain that contained horse-radish. His court papers state that the stain on the knife was blood. Hobart is petitioning the court to perform a DNA test on the blood from the knife. He argues that the blood from two sources will be found—Marilyn Jones and Geoff Slate. Hobart claims that the knife was purposely contaminated with another man's blood to try to link Hobart to the scene. Hobart has reason to believe it is her current boyfriend, Geoff Slate.

Richmond Superior Court Judge John Steiner has ruled that a new round of forensic tests be done. He has ordered:

- Retesting of the stain on the cloth found at Hobart's apartment.
- A determination if the stain is human blood.
- An STR DNA analysis of the blood on the knife to determine if any of the blood matches Steve Hobart, Marilyn Jones, and/or Geoff Slate.
- Submission of known DNA evidence samples from Marilyn Jones, Steve Hobart, and Geoff Slate.

Judge Steiner has asked that the report, if possible, answer these questions:

- Is the cloth recovered by police at Hobart's residence stained with blood or some other substance?

- Can the blood on the knife be matched to any of the three individuals?

What You Need:

- an adult
- safety glasses
- polyethylene gloves
- kitchen funnel
- spray bottle
- 2 tablespoons
- luminol (from your science teacher)
- calcium carbonate (12 antacid tablets, e.g., extra-strength TUMS®)
- distilled water
- measuring cup
- hydrogen peroxide [H_2O_2], 3 percent (from drug store)
- pen with indelible ink
- vinegar
- 3 paper cups
- gauze sheet, 12-inch square
- horseradish root (from a grocery store)
- kitchen blender
- red and blue food coloring
- 4 x 6-inch cotton cloth or handkerchief
- 2 eyedroppers
- phenolphthalein, in dropping bottle (from a pool supply store)
- toothpick
- Table 8 DNA evidence profiles (STR analysis)
- ruler
- notebook
- access to a photocopier
- a friend who will be the investigator

What You Do:

MAKE AND USE TEST SOLUTIONS

Luminol Test Solution

(Make just before use; see Case #6.)

1. Place a kitchen funnel onto a spray bottle with the spray head removed.

2. Measure 0.3 grams (1/8 teaspoon) of luminol. Pour the measured luminol into the funnel. (You will flush it, and other chemicals, down into the bottle in a later step.)

3. Measure 13 grams (approximately 12 Extra-strength Tums tablets at 1.11 g per tablet) of calcium carbonate. Crush each tablet between two spoons. Pour the powder into the funnel.

4. Measure 250 mL (1 cup) of distilled water. Pour it into the funnel to dissolve the solid chemicals.

5. Measure 250 mL (1 cup) of 3 percent hydrogen peroxide solution. Pour it into the funnel to dissolve the solid chemicals. Remove the funnel. Replace the spray head. Carefully shake the bottle to mix the chemicals. Let the solids settle, and avoid spraying any undissolved chemical. Label the spray bottle "Luminol Solution."

Precipitin Test Solution

1. Label a small paper cup "Precipitin Test Solution."
2. Pour a small amount (15 mL) of vinegar into the cup.
   - Kastle-Meyer Peroxidase Test Solutions

3. Label a small paper cup "3 percent Hydrogen Peroxide Solution."

4. Pour a small amount (15 mL) of 3 percent hydrogen peroxide into the cup.

SETTING UP THE EVIDENCE

1. Fold a 12-inch-square sheet of gauze into a 4 x 4-inch square. Place the gauze square over a paper cup.

2. **With adult permission**, use a kitchen blender to grind up about 5 inches of fresh horseradish root. Use a tablespoon to scoop the ground-up horseradish root and place it in the gauze. Press on the material to squeeze the root juice into the cup. Also pour any juice from the blender through the gauze filter. After filtering, discard the gauze and root material.

3. Add 10 to 15 drops of red food coloring, mixed with 1–2 drops of blue food coloring to the horseradish root juice in the cup. Mix the materials with the spoon to produce a reddish-brown color similar to barbeque sauce.

4. Use an eyedropper to apply this simulated barbeque sauce onto a clean 4 x 6-inch cotton cloth. Allow the stain to dry. Re-apply the simulated barbeque sauce to the same area at least two or three times to concentrate the peroxidase enzyme, an enzyme in the horseradish.

5. Make a photocopy of Table 9 for your friend to analyze.

ANALYZE THE STAINED CLOTH

Have a friend be the criminalist investigating the case. Remind your friend to refer to the background information on blood analysis in Chapter 2, and in Cases #1 and #2.

1. Have your friend perform an examination of the stained cloth that the Court has ordered. Is the stain blood? Is it human blood?

2. Record the test results in your notebook.

ANALYZE STR DNA RESULTS

1. Have your friend make an analysis of the data contained in Table 8. It summarizes the STR analysis results for:
   - Marilyn Jones, victim (known)
   - Steve Hobart, accused (known)
   - Geoff Slate, suspect (known)
   - knife (unknown)

2. Your friend's analysis should clarify whether there is blood from one or two individuals on the knife. Can an identity be made? Can any individual be eliminated?

WRITE A REPORT TO THE COURT

Judge Steiner would like the report to include:
   - description of the tests done on the physical evidence
   - summary of results
   - findings of fact (See Judge Steiner's questions on pages 80–81.)

TABLE 8. DNA Evidence Profiles
(STR Analysis)

Sample	Marking (Sample number)	Gender	DNA Markers and Alleles: Hobart Case								
			D3	D8	D21	D18	D5	D13	D7	FGA	vWA
Slate	S-1	Male XY	17/18	8/8	35.2/36	27/27	7/8	8/14	7/8	16/30.2	21/21
Hobart	S-2	Male XY	9/10	8/11	28.2/30.2	21/27	9/9	8/8	7/9	12/16	24/43.2
Jones	V	Female XX	16/16	10/14	26/31	11/14	12/13	8/13	7/7	30/30	15/19
Knife	M-1	X, Y	16/17/18	8/10/14	26/31/35.2/36	11/14/27	7/8/12/13	8/13/14	7/8	16/30/30.2	15/19/21

- whether any individual can be excluded or included
- whether any unusual results need further explanation

Compare the findings to those in the Analysis section (Chapter 7) of this book.

Case Analyses

This chapter contains analysis findings for each of the cases and projects presented in this book.

CHAPTER 3

CASE #1. **The Case of the Overlooked Stain**

Science Project Idea:

Plants contain peroxidase that can give a false positive Kastle-Meyer test result. Plants that contain a large amount of peroxidase include: potato, horseradish, lima bean, pine, tomato, turnip, rutabaga, tree (e.g., pine) saps, fruit juices (concentrate), and green beans.

CASE #2. **The Case of the Stain in Question**

PROJECT: **Testing for Human Blood**

Analysis Findings:

The simulated bloodstain in "Blood Evidence Sample #1" is colored water. The reaction between vinegar and the yellow water produced a negative precipitin reaction. The simulated bloodstain in "Blood Evidence Sample #2" contains heavy cream and red-colored water. The reaction between vinegar and heavy cream will produce white flakes of clumped milk protein.

These white clumps simulate a positive precipitin reaction.

● ● ● ● ● ● ● ● ● ● ● ● ● ● ● ● ●

CASE #3. The Case of the Almost
Perfect Murder

PROJECT: Creating Bloodstain Patterns

Analysis Findings:

- Figure 13 shows impact bloodstains on a smooth surface (such as tile or glass) at heights of 6 inches, 1 foot, 4 feet, and 7 feet. A blood drop on a smooth surface will show hardly any distortion. It will have few spines or spatter.
- Blood drops that strike a rough surface at 90 degrees (such as construction paper) are circular. Their diameter ranges in size from 8 to 16 millimeters based on the height of its fall.

FIGURE 13

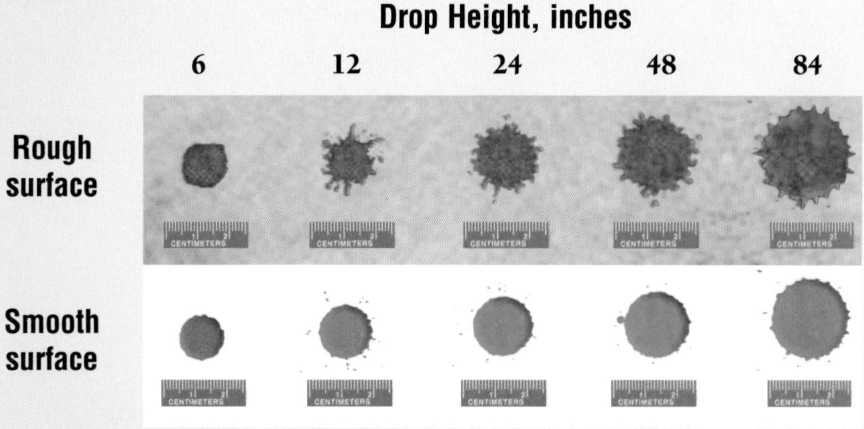

Drop Height, inches

| 6 | 12 | 24 | 48 | 84 |

Rough surface

Smooth surface

Blood drop diameter increases as the height from which it drops increases, up to a height of seven feet (84 inches).

87

- Blood drops falling on a rough, textured surface will show star-shaped spines and edge spatter due to the disruption of the surface.
- The size of a free-falling blood drop increases with the distance that it has fallen, up to about 7 feet. At distances beyond 7 feet, the diameter of the bloodstains does not increase.
- Blood drops do not break up before they hit a surface, even from great heights.
- A blood drop stain becomes more elliptical (oval) as its angle of impact decreases from perpendicular (90 degrees).

• • • • • • • • • • • • • • • • • • • •

CASE #4. The Case of the Speckled T-shirt

PROJECT: Locating the Point of Origin in a Bloodstain Pattern

Analysis Findings:

Table 9 summarizes impact angle calculations. Figure 14 illustrates the point of origin of the bloodstain pattern.

FIGURE 14

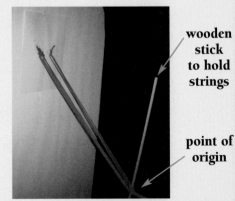

wooden stick to hold strings

point of origin

Strings from the center of individual blood drops are extended at corresponding impact angles to join at the point of origin. The point of origin is the area in space where the blood originated.

TABLE 9. Analysis: Impact Angle Calculations

Drop Number	Width (mm)	Length (mm)	W/L Ratio	Impact Angle (From Figure 4)
1	2	13	0.15	8 degrees
2	2.5	8	0.31	15 degrees
3	2.8	8.5	0.33	18 degrees
4	3	7	0.43	21 degrees
5	4	8	0.5	30 degrees
6	3	9	0.33	18 degrees
7	4.6	11.2	0.41	22 degrees
8	4.1	10.5	0.39	20 degrees
9	4	7.5	0.53	30 degrees
10	3.4	6.2	0.55	32 degrees

CASE #5: The Case of the Telling Trapdoor

PROJECT: Analyzing Blood Stain Patterns

Analysis Findings:

- The blood drop splash pattern is not distorted and is consistent with drops falling on a smooth surface—there are very little spatter spines.
- The height from which the drops fell ranged from two to four feet (Table 10).
- Drops fell at an angle of 90 degrees. This is consistent with passive drops forming and dripping off an object. The drops are not projected castoffs. They do not have the appearance of being flung off an object.

TABLE 10. Analysis: Bloodstain Pattern

Drop #	Drop Diameter (mm)	Fall Height (Feet)
1	9	2+
2	9.5	2+
3	9.5	2+
4	9.5	2+
5	9	2+
6	9	2+
7	9.5	2+
8	9	2+
9	—	—
10	—	—
11	10	3
12	10.5	4

- The total volume of blood found was very small—0.6 mL (12 drops having an average volume of 0.05 mL each). The physical evidence agrees with the husband's statement: Drop heights from 2+ feet (28 inches) indicate that the injured hand hung straight down. Larger-sized drops indicate that the man held his injured hand at waist height (about three feet) or higher.

Science Project Idea

Cast-off spatter tends to be oval or elliptical in shape as the weapon is swung in an arc—either overhead or to the side. Cast-off droplets are more round as it approaches a 90-degree angle over the attacker's head (see Figure 15).

FIGURE 15

FIGURE 15

This is the appearance of blood drops at points along the arc of a swinging arm, from which blood spatters.

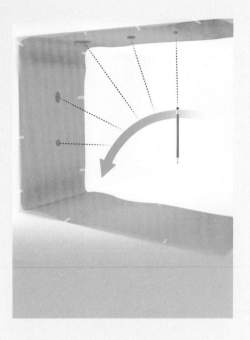

●●●●●●●●●●●●●●●●

CASE #6: The Case of the Glowing Light

PROJECT: Detecting Trace Amounts of Blood

Analysis Findings:

- The red color disappears below a concentration of 1/1,000 (cap 3).
- The luminol reagent can detect the presence of the simulated blood spilled on a cloth at concentrations up to 1/1,000,000 (cap 6).

●●●●●●●●●●●●●●●●●●●●

CHAPTER 5

CASE #7: The Case of the False Conviction

PROJECT: Excluding Suspects Using STR DNA Analysis

Analysis Findings:

- All blood samples on the cloth, mallet, awl, and coat were from male. Because the sample on the mallet is a mixture, it could be from males or a male/female mixture.
- The wood mallet (M-2) was contaminated with blood from two individuals—Treadwell and the victim. Confirmation that the wooden mallet is the murder weapon would be made upon further study of the body.
- The awl (M-3) is contaminated with blood from Treadwell.
- The coat (M-4) was contaminated with blood from the victim.
- The cloth (M-1) was contaminated with blood from Treadwell.
- Based upon STR analysis:
  - An STR MATCH shows that the awl (M-3) was mixed with Treadwell's blood. This physical evidence points to the victim defending himself with an awl, inflicting a blood-drawing wound on Treadwell.
  - An STR MATCH shows that the cloth (M-1) was mixed with Treadwell's blood. The bloodstain is concentrated in one area. This evidence suggests that Treadwell used a bandana to stop the flow of blood from a wound created by the awl.
  - The STR analysis shows a match of both the victim's and Treadwell's blood to the mallet

(M-2). This mixing of DNA links Treadwell to the victim.

- Roberts can be excluded from association with any blood-contaminated article, including the murder weapon. There is NO STR match between Roberts and any article found at the crime scene.

- Alderson can be excluded because there is no STR match between Alderson and any article found at the crime scene.

●●●●●●●●●●●●●●●●●●

CHAPTER 6

The Case of the Second Examination

Analysis Findings:

1. Stained Cloth
   - Kastle-Meyer test is positive: bubbling.
   - Luminol test may be positive.
   - Precipitin test is negative.

The Kastle-Meyer test was positive. The stain is biological-either from blood or plant cells. The luminol test may be positive, indicating that the stain is biological—either from blood or plant cells. The precipitin test is negative. The stain is not human blood.

Hobart stated in court papers that the cloth was stained with barbeque sauce that contained horseradish. The presence of bubbles with the application of hydrogen peroxide and the possible bluish glow from the application of the luminol solution supports this statement. A second peroxidase test (hydrogen peroxide) on horseradish juice (a control) gave the same results (bubbling).

Hobart's claim that the stain on the recovered cloth was not blood is verified.

2. Bloody Knife

- The knife is contaminated with two sources of blood (male and female) that are mixed together. Allele matches to Geoff Slate and the victim, Marilyn Jones, occur for all nine DNA markers. For example, marker D3 shows alleles 16, 17, and 18 found on the knife. The victim has two 16 alleles; Slate has the 17, 18 alleles.
- Steve Hobart can be excluded as there is only one match (D13) for his nine DNA markers.

Summary of Findings:

Steve Hobart's court testimony is truthful. The cloth found in his apartment is not stained with blood, but with barbeque sauce. Marilyn Jones' and Geoff Slate's blood were found on the knife. Steve Hobart cannot be forensically linked to the alleged assault.

GLOSSARY

adenine—One of the four bases in a DNA molecule; adenine (A) pairs with thymine (T).

allele—One of a pair of genes that occupy a specific position on a specific chromosome.

amino acids—Molecules that are the building blocks of proteins.

angle of impact—the angle (acute) between the direction of the blood drop and the plane of the surface it strikes.

base—Portion of a nucleotide molecule that makes it an A, G, T, C.

base pair (bp)—In double-stranded DNA, a nucleotide base and its complement.

blood—A fluid (plasma) containing red cells, white cells, and platelets. Red cells carry the protein hemoglobin that gives blood its red color.

bloodstain—evidence that blood has come into contact with an object or surface.

blood serum—Sticky, watery liquid left after the solid parts of the blood (the red blood cells, white blood cells, and platelets) have clumped (coagulated).

cast-off pattern—bloodstain pattern caused by blood being released from an object in motion.

cell—Basic structural unit of an organism.

chemiluminescence—The generation of light without heat through a chemical reaction.

chromosome—The structure by which hereditary information is physically transmitted from one generation to the next; the cell structure that carries the genes.

CODIS—*Combined DNA Index System.* A series of local, state, and national computer applications and databases administered by the FBI.

cytosine—One of the four bases that combines with a sugar and a phosphate to form a nucleotide subunit of DNA; cytosine (C) pairs with guanine (G).

deoxyribonucleic acid (DNA)—The genetic material of organisms. It is made of two chains of nucleotides in the form of a double helix.

DNA amplification—A process of copying DNA to greatly increase its amount for testing and analysis.

DNA database—A group of DNA profiles that allow comparison. Usually stored electronically. *See also* CODIS.

DNA extraction—A process by which DNA is removed and purified from cells.

DNA profiling—A process used to distinguish between individuals of the same species using samples of their DNA.

enzyme—A protein that makes it possible for certain chemical reactions to occur quickly.

evidence sample—Sample for which the origin is unknown. Usually taken from the crime scene, or people or objects associated with it.

gene—The basic unit of heredity; a sequence of DNA nucleotides on a chromosome. Genes are passed from parent to offspring.

GLOSSARY

• • •

genome—The total genetic makeup of an organism.

genotype—The specific genes present in an organism.

guanine—One of the four bases that combine with a sugar and a phosphate to form a nucleotide subunit of DNA; guanine (G) pairs with cytosine (C).

laser—A device that converts mixed types of light into a single, highly amplified type.

locus (*plural loci*)—The location on a chromosome where the gene for a particular trait is located.

nucleotide—A unit of nucleic acid made up of a sugar, a phosphate, and one of four bases. The raw building blocks of DNA.

nucleus—The membrane-covered organelle found in most cells; contains the cell's DNA organized into chromosomes. It serves as the control center for the cell.

parent drop—A drop of blood from which a wave cast-off, or satellite spatter.

PCR (polymerase chain reaction)—A technique of using DNA polymerase (an enzyme) to make many copies of DNA for further analysis and testing.

plasma—The colorless, watery liquid portion of blood.

polymorphism—The ability to appear in many forms. In STR DNA analysis, it means the number of times a 4-nucleotide sequence is repeated (e.g., number of copies) at a specific chromosome location that occurs in a population of individuals.

protein—A type of biological molecule that is made up of amino acids. They provide much of the body's structure and function. Enzymes are a type of protein.

serology—The branch of forensic science concerned with the study of the body fluids.

spatter—Coverage pattern of a surface by drops of blood from an object or by gravitational force.

spine—Pointed or elongated stains that flow away from the central area of a bloodstain when it strikes the surface at an angle.

STR (short tandem repeat) DNA analysis—The most widely used DNA profiling procedures. During forensic examination, an STR is extracted, amplified, and separated using gel electrophoresis. The separated DNA is scanned by a laser, displayed, and compared to other STRs in a computer display called an electropherogram.

thymine—One of the four bases that combine with a sugar and a phosphate to form a nucleotide subunit of DNA; thymine (T) pairs with adenine (A).

wave cast-off—A small blood drop that originates from a parent drop of blood that flows from the parent drop as it strikes the surface.

APPENDIX
Science Supply Companies

Most of the materials required for investigations in this book are available at local stores. Items such as phenolphthalein solution and luminol can be obtained from the sources below. Most companies can be contacted on the Internet; some have online catalogs that will make direct ordering easy.

1 Carolina Biological
Supply Company
2700 York Road
Burlington, NC 27215
(800) 227-1150
http://www.carolina.com

2 Connecticut Valley Biological
Supply Company
P.O. Box 326
82 Valley Road
South Hampton, MA 01703
(800) 628-7748
http://www.ctvalleybio.com

3 Delta Education
80 Northwest Blvd.
P.O. Box 3000
Nashua, NH 03061-3000
(800) 442-5444
http://www.delta-education.com/

4 Discovery Scope® Inc.
Easy-to-use single lens microscope.
3202 Echo Mountain Dr.
Kingwood, TX 77345
http://www.Discoveryscope.com

5 Fisher Science Education
485 South Frontage Road
Burr Ridge, IL 60521
(800) 955-1177
http://www.fisheredu.com

6 Flinn Scientific
P.O. Box 219
Batavia, IL 60510-0219
(800) 452-1261
http://www.flinnsci.com

7 Frey Scientific
P.O. Box 8101
100 Paragon Parkway
Mansfield, OH 44903
(800) 225-3739
http://www.freyscientific.com

8 Neo/SCI Corporation
P.O. Box 22729
100 Aviation Avenue
Rochester, NY 14692-2729
(800) 526-6689
http://www.neosci.com

FURTHER READING

BOOKS

Conklin, Barbara Gardner, Robert Gardner, and Dennis Shortelle. *Encyclopedia of Forensic Science: A Compendium of Detective Fact and Fiction*. Westport, Conn.: Oryx Press, 2002.

Fridell, Ron. *DNA Fingerprinting: The Ultimate Identity*. New York: Franklin Watts, 2001.

———. *Solving Crimes: Pioneers of Forensic Science*. New York: Franklin Watts, 2000.

Morgan, Marilyn. *Careers in Criminology*. New York: McGraw-Hill, 2000.

Owen, David. *Police Lab: How Forensic Science Tracks Down and Convicts Criminals*. Buffalo, N.Y.: Firefly Books Ltd., 2002.

Platt, Richard. *Crime Scene: The Ultimate Guide to Forensic Science*. London: Dorling Kindersley, Ltd., 2003.

Rainis, Kenneth G. *Crime-Solving Science Projects. Forensic Science Experiments*. Berkeley Heights, N.J.: Enslow Publishers, Inc., 2000.

Ramsland, Katherine. *The Forensic Science of C.S.I.* San Francisco: Berkley Publishing Group, 2001.

INTERNET ADDRESSES

CourtTV.com. Forensics in the Classroom. © 2002. <http://www.courttv.com/forensics_curriculum>

Federal Bureau of Investigation. FBI Youth. <http://www.fbi.gov/kids/6th12th/6th12th.htm>

INDEX

ABOUT THE AUTHOR

Kenneth G. Rainis is a microbiologist, illustrator, and microscopist, as well as a cofounder of Neo/Sci Corporation, a science education company in New York. He has a B.S. in biology and an M.S. in protozoology. He has authored numerous science labs and science project books. Mr. Rainis is also a contributor, reviewer, and safety consultant for a number of high school and college biology textbooks. He lives in New York with his wife and children.